THE SUDDEN IN THE SCRIPTURES

THE SUDDEN IN THE SCRIPTURES

BY

DAVID DAUBE

LEIDEN
E. J. BRILL
1964

PRINTED IN THE NETHERLANDS

To

PETER and JANET

CONTENTS

CHAPTER ONE

THE OLD TESTAMENT AND RABBINIC LITERATURE *

I. PITH'OM AND PETHA'

a) *General*

There are two words in Old Testament Hebrew exclusively used in the sense of 'suddenly', *pith'om* and *petha'*. They are synonymous, and in four texts they are joined as a double expression, 'very suddenly'.[1] With one or two questionable exceptions, [2] they always occur in connection with disaster. They would be out of place in the Song of Solomon.

This bias is largely explicable on realistic grounds. As we look at objects and beings, destruction is in fact likely to be swifter than creation. It takes time to build a house, but it may collapse in a moment. Human birth follows a pregnancy of nine months, but an apoplexy comes out of the blue. Furthermore, it is the unexpected that hits you, gives you a jolt, which is called 'sudden'; and the unexpected that hits you is more often than not of an unpleasant nature — if only because we incline to take the pleasurable (or the absence of the unpleasant) for granted. We are more forcibly struck by the abrupt onset of a headache than its abrupt disappearance. There is indeed, for many people, something worrying in the unexpected as such: one might hear a man declare, 'I do not like surprises' (*ich liebe keine Überraschungen*), expressing an indiscriminate aversion to what is not planned, even though beneficial. That dangers are easier to meet if mentally prepared for is stated by Aristotle: 'It is the mark of a braver man to be fearless in sudden (*aiphnidios*) fears than in those anticipated; what is anticipated one may face by reasoning, the sudden (*exaiphnes*) according to character'.[3] In insecure times—among which for the present purpose we may include the entire Old Testament period—distrust

---

*) N.B. Some aspects of the subject are elaborated in Suddenness and Awe in Scripture, Tenth (1963) Robert Waley Cohen Memorial Lecture, London, 1964.

[1] Nu 6.9, Is 29.5, 30.13, Si 11.21.
[2] II Chr 29.36, Si 11.21; see below, pp. 7ff.   [3] Nic. Eth. 3.8.15.

of the unforeseen is bound to be greater than in times of comparative security. That (in addition to normal wear and tear) is behind the gradual relaxation of the meaning of *pith'om* and *petha'*: in post-Biblical Hebrew, we shall see, they are no longer tied to misfortune.

The foregoing considerations are admittedly of so general a character that they ought to be valid for other languages as well. They are, *mutatis mutandis*. In fact, the evidence from other languages confirms that the development in Hebrew is not due to some accident of transmission. In the Latin *subitus*, for instance, the *sub* indicates a disagreeable, uncanny element (though possibly the idea of one thing following upon another is also present). In Italian, the adverb *subito* means no more than 'directly', while 'suddenly' nowadays has its nearest equivalent in *improvvisamente* or the like; in Spanish, on the other hand, *subito* still means 'suddenly'. German *plötzlich* has to do with *platzen*, 'explosion' (related to *plaudere*), *Blitz*, *auf dem Platz*, all originally uncomfortable things. In modern English we can certainly say 'suddenly I noticed my girl', 'the solution of the problem came to me by a sudden revelation', as well as 'he died a sudden death', 'suddenly he fell', 'suddenly the alarm rang out'. But a glance through the quotations in the Oxford Dictionary will shew that the word starts in association with terror and gradually becomes neutral. (The case of 'stroke' comes to mind. We speak of 'a stroke of luck', but when this phrase was coined—in the 19th century—it was no doubt a paradox.) Even today, if one looked for 'sudden' in titles of books, one would have a better chance with the green Penguin series than the red one.

However, we are not claiming that this realistic background alone accounts for the restriction of *pith'om* and *petha'* to the sphere of evil. There are additional factors of which the most important is familiar from many comparable cases: it will emerge that, once the two words had been prominently employed in certain contexts, that fact itself made for continued usage along the same lines, at the expense of other potentialities. (The tension between this tendency and what we described above as wear and tear is a common phenomenon.) Especially in literary style, a traditional prevalence of 'sudden' in, say, invocations of evil on one's enemies or in warnings concerning the last judgment, might well contribute to a narrowing of the range.

Etymological considerations we shall leave on one side, if only

because there is too little certainty. Are *pith'om* and *petha᷄* from
the same root? Accadian *pitta, pittimma, ina pitta* and so on—
'instant, 'instantly' or 'suddenly'—may well be related and would
be worth comparing; but the relevant volume of the Chicago
Dictionary is not yet available. The root *b᷄t*, expressing the seizure
of a man by some terror, is claimed to be identical, originally, with
petha᷄.[1] This would greatly strengthen our case. An out-of-date
derivation by Gesenius will be mentioned at the end of this essay.[2]

b) *The texts*

Let us inspect the evidence. From the Pentateuch only three
passages are to be listed, all in Numbers. A Nazarite may not come
into contact with a corpse; and 'if any man die very suddenly by
him', he must bring a sacrifice.[3] Another law is designed to mitigate
vengeance where a man killed another man unwittingly, 'thrust
him suddenly, without enmity'.[4]

Thirdly, as Aaron and Miriam rebelled against Moses, 'the Lord
spake suddenly unto Moses and Aaron and Miriam, Come out ye
three'.[5] God appeared as judge, the summons was a threat; so the
term has its usual implications. But we find here, what we shall
find again and again, that where it is a question of opposing par-
ties, a certain ambiguity tends to creep in: what is dreadful for
one may be welcome to the other. *Dem einen sein Tod ist dem andern
sein Brot.* Moses on the present occasion was vindicated by God.
By making the latter speak 'suddenly', the narrative emphasizes
the effect of the intervention on the guilty brother and sister; and,
of course, at this moment Moses himself does not yet know what is
to happen. It remains none the less true that this 'sudden' intervention brought him deliverance.

Two passages in Joshua. Joshua made a forced night march
against the Amorite kings and 'came upon them suddenly';[6] and
similarly, in the case of the king of Hazor and his allies, 'Joshua
and all the people of war with him came upon them suddenly and
fell upon them'.[7] Again, the 'suddenly' looks at it from the point

---

[1] Professor T. H. Gaster kindly drew my attention to this point.
[2] See below, p. 78.
[3] Nu 6.9, with the double expression *bephetha᷄ pith'om*.
[4] Nu 35.22.
[5] Nu 12.4.
[6] Jo 10.9.
[7] Jo 11.7.

of view of the victim. These affairs were anything but fearful for Joshua.

Isaiah predicts the overthrow of Sennacherib in one gruesome night: 'The multitude of thy terrible ones shall be as chaff that passeth away, yea it shall be very suddenly'.[1] Here, too, the reference is primarily to the impact on the enemy—his discomfiture, however, is Jerusalem's salvation. It is interesting that, in giving warning of Sennacherib's forthcoming incursion, Isaiah also uses the term, this time from the point of view of Jerusalem: 'Therefore this iniquity shall be to you as a breach ready to fall, swelling out in a high wall, whose breaking cometh very suddenly'.[2]

Babylon's defeat at the hand of Cyrus is announced in Deutero-Isaiah: 'Mischief shall fall upon thee, and desolation shall come upon thee suddenly, thou shalt not know.'[3] Very likely it is this event which is recalled in the passage: 'I declared the former things from the beginning, and out of my mouth they went forth and I shewed them; suddenly I did them and they came'.[4]

Jeremiah warns his people: 'Breaking upon breaking is cried, suddenly my tents are spoiled and my curtains in a moment.'[5] 'The spoiler shall suddenly come upon us.'[6] 'I have caused a spoiler to come to them, upon the mother of the young men, at noonday; I have caused him to fall upon her suddenly'.[7] 'Let a cry be heard from their houses when thou shalt cause a troop to come upon them suddenly'.[8] The word also occurs in a prophecy of doubtful authorship, against Babylon: 'Babylon is suddenly fallen and broken.'[9] In all these cases the 'sudden' ruin of one party coincides with the triumph of the other—not to mention the role of God, standing above both.

Retribution will overtake the ruthless, according to Habakkuk: 'Shall they not rise up suddenly that shall bite thee?'.[10] Malachi's proclamation of the judgment is famous: 'And the Lord, whom ye

---

[1] Is 29.5, *lephetha^c pith^ɔom*.
[2] Is 30.13, *pith^ɔom lephetha^c*.
[3] Is 47.11.
[4] Is 48.3.
[5] Jer 4.20.
[6] Jer 6.26.
[7] Jer 15.8.
[8] Jer 18.22.
[9] Jer 51.8.
[10] Hab 2.7.

seek, shall suddenly come to his temple'.[1] The clause 'whom ye
seek' is ironical, the idea being that of Amos: 'Woe unto you that
desire the day of the Lord; the day of the Lord is darkness and not
light'.[2] The very use of 'suddenly' points this way, but we need
only read on to find it confirmed. For Malachi continues: 'And
who may abide the day of his coming? and who shall stand when
he appeareth?'.[3] However, the ambiguity to which we have repeatedly adverted is not absent: the judgment, 'sudden' and terrible
as it is for the haughty sinners, will at the same time vindicate
those oppressed by them, the fatherless, the widows, the strangers.

In Psalm 64, while the wicked ones use calumny as arrows against
the author—who is good—and 'suddenly shoot at him', God 'shall
shoot at them with a sudden arrow'.[4] Here it is very evident how
what for one party is a blow, 'sudden', is welcome to the other.
The Psalm ends: 'The righteous shall rejoice in the Lord' and so
on.[5]

Proverbs contains several relevant passages. The wise disciple
may be confident: 'Be not afraid of sudden terror, neither of the
desolation of the wicked when it cometh'.[6] As for the false man,
'suddenly shall come his calamity, suddenly shall he be broken
without remedy'.[7] Of two unreliable types of men we are told:
'For suddenly shall rise up their calamity, and the ruin of them
both who shall know?'[8] Again, 'he that hardeneth his neck shall
suddenly be broken, and that without remedy'.[9]

In a last text from Proverbs,[10] *pith'om* is a different word from
that under review. More precisely, it belongs to *patha* or *pethi*,

---

[1] Mal 3.1.

[2] Am 5.18.

[3] Mal 3.2.

[4] Ps 64.5, 8. The latter verse is hardly intact, but the general sense is clear.

[5] Ps 64.11.

[6] Pr 3.25. The verse is alluded to at the end of I Pet 3.6: good women need not fear. Quite possibly the author here is still thinking of Sarah. In the first half of 3.6 she is held up as a model because she called her husband 'lord' (Gen 18.12). But on that same occasion she committed a wrong (laughing at the annunciation of a son) which, challenged, she feared to admit (Gen 18.15). The end of 3.6 may well mean: 'whose children ye are, doing good only, however, and therefore not fearing with any scare'.

[7] Pr 6.15.

[8] Pr 24.22; hardly intact.

[9] Pr 29.1.

[10] Pr 7.22; see commentaries and dictionaries.

'compliant', 'simple', and is either an exceptionally formed adverb or in need of slight emendation. (The LXX assumes *patha* or *pethi* instead of *pith'om* in two texts besides the present one,[1] and we shall presently suggest an emendation along these lines for a passage from Chronicles.[2] In the Zadokite Fragments such an emendation is widely accepted.[3]) The section deals with a young man's seduction by a loose woman: 'He goeth after her in his simplicity, as an ox goeth to the slaughter'. In any case, in the view of the author, the young man is in for disaster—so the text suits our general thesis with or without emendation. We must, however, append a reservation. Though the original reference is to 'simple-mindedness', in course of time, as 'suddenly' was losing its fearful connotation, readers might think of this adverb in interpreting the text.[4] This tendency would be encouraged by the picture—also dating from a period when the term had become less sinister— of the fool as one who acts 'suddenly', in an erratic, abrupt fashion.[5] To be sure, even the fool's 'suddenness' is ultimately ruinous in the literature in question.

One of Job's friends, Eliphaz, says: 'I have seen the foolish taking root, but suddenly I cursed his habitation'.[6] That this envisages a dramatic fall is clear. Possibly we should translate 'I found his habitation cursed', 'I had to declare, call, his habitation cursed'; the opposite of *'ishsher*, 'to praise, call, happy'. Eliphaz also tells Job that it is for his moral shortcomings that 'sudden terror troubleth thee'.[7] Job himself sees God equally thwarting the good and the bad: 'If the scourge slay suddenly, he will laugh at the trial of the innocent'.[8]

For Ecclesiastes, too, things happen without rhyme or reason: 'The race is not to the swift nor the battle to the strong neither yet the bread to the wise. For man also knoweth not his time: as the fishes that are taken in an evil net, so are the sons of men snared

---

[1] See below, p. 12.
[2] II Chr 29.36; see below, pp. 7f.
[3] Zad Fr 14.2; see below, pp. 21f.
[4] See below, pp. 13, 20f., on the renderings of Aquila, Symmachus and, above all, the Targum.
[5] See below, pp. 13ff., 24f., on the variant *aphno* in the LXX, Ec 10.3, on *exapina* in Lev 21.4, Nu 4.20, and on Rabbinic disquisitions concerning the sudden (*pith'om*) entry of a house.
[6] Job 5.3.
[7] Job 22.10.
[8] Job 9.23.

in an evil time when it falleth suddenly upon them'.[1] In Job, the complaint is about God's indifference to ethics: the good is treated no better than the bad. In Ecclesiastes, it is about fate making nonsense of human faculties. This does not indeed mean that the ethical problem is foreign to Ecclesiastes. It is just a little below the surface—as in the song from the Dreigroschenoper: *Ja mach nur einen Plan, sei nur ein grosses Licht, und mach noch einen zweiten Plan—gehn tun sie beide nicht.*

This leaves a single text in the canonical Old Testament[2] where 'suddenly' is associated with a happy event: the Chronicler, after describing the rededication of the Temple by Hezekiah, adds, 'And Hezekiah rejoiced and all the people over what God had prepared for the people, for the thing took place suddenly'. To be sure, the rededication involved elimination and destruction of impure objects,[3] but this aspect is not in the foreground in the jubilant concluding remark quoted. A possible explanation is that, by the time of Chronicles, the word had become neutral enough to be suitable for any striking, unexpected, fast-occurring incident. But there is room for doubt. The form *bephith'om* (with the particle *be*, 'in', 'with') is unique in the Old Testament and very rare even in post-Biblical literature.[4] It is probably, however, unobjectionable: *bephetha'*, after all, occurs three times.[5] What is of greater weight is that it is far from obvious how to understand 'suddenly': does it refer to the unexpected change of policy after Ahaz?, or to the fact that Hezekiah undertook the reform immediately on accession?, or to the speed with which it was carried through?, or to what? Maybe recourse should be had to an emendation similar to that mentioned above:[6] we might read *bappetha'im* or *biphetha'im*— which would touch none of the consonants, only the vocalisation. 'For the thing took place among (the) simple ones'.[7] In doctrine, the passage would be allied to others where God grants special

---

[1] Ec 9.11 f.

[2] II Chr 29.36; on Sirach, see presently, p. 8.

[3] II Chr 29.16.

[4] It is met, e.g., in Bab. Shabbath 153a, to be discussed below, p. 23, but even here the Munich MS at least has *pith'om*.

[5] Nu 6.9, 35.22, Si 11.21; in the first and third of these *bephetha' pith'om*.

[6] In connection with Pr 7.22; see pp. 5f.

[7] The form *bappetha'yim* occurs in Pr 7.7, concerning a young man's seduction: 'And I beheld among the simple ones a young man void of understanding'.

protection and enlightenment to 'the simple', to those who, however weak, liable to error, inadequate, are eager to do his will.[1] It should be observed that, in the verses directly preceding the concluding remark under discussion, we learn that as the ritual could not be performed exactly as it ought to have been (because there were not enough priests), it was performed in the nearest possible fashion.[2]

It is universally assumed that *pith'om* and *petha'* have a pleasant sense also in Sirach. *Pith'om* occurs three times, twice plainly of disaster: as a sinner, do not (Sirach warns you) delay repentance, 'for suddenly doth his wrath come forth';[3] and ill-gotten gain or its owner 'shall suddenly perish for ever'.[4] But there is another maxim, to the effect that God may 'very suddenly make a poor man rich'.[5] Box and Oesterley adopt Edersheim's verdict, that 'the moral of this verse can scarcely be considered elevated'.[6] But though the Greek does give this text, the Hebrew is defective: the portion 'make a poor man rich' is not there. The presence of 'suddenly' rather militates against this reconstruction.

That Sirach adheres to the archaic restriction of the term is suggested by his warning against the unannounced, inconsiderate entering of a house. Whereas a Talmudic allusion to it has *pith'om*, a more reliable quotation in a Midrashic work has 'hastily', 'soon', *mehera*: 'The foot of a fool is soon into a house'.[7] The Talmudic passage contains matter plainly not represented in Sirach; the Midrashic version is superior. It may be worth adding, in view of Rabbinic sayings to be mentioned below,[8] that Sirach is thinking of entering somebody else's house, not one's own.

---

[1] Ps 116.6, 119.30. Ez 45.20 prescribes an annual cleansing of the Temple 'from a man that erreth and from a simple one'. Cp., possibly, from the Dead Sea Scrolls, Habakkuk 12.4f., where 'the beasts' of the original (Hab 2.17) are interpreted as 'the simple ones of Judah, the doers of the Torah'.

[2] II Chr 29.34f. Cp. II Chr 30.17f., a very similar situation at Hezekiah's Passover.

[3] Si 5.7.

[4] Si 40.14.

[5] Si 11.21, with the double *bephetha' pith'om*.

[6] Charles, Apocrypha and Pseudepigrapha, 1913, vol. 1, 355.

[7] Si 21.22; Greek *tachys*. See Bab. Nidda 16b, Pirqa deRabenu Haqadosh, Baba deShisha 4, ed. Schönblum, 1877, 14a. Schönblum, however, did not spot the provenance of the quotation: that was discovered later.

[8] See pp. 24f.

2. REGHA‘

Besides *pith'om* and *petha‘*, it is necessary to look at *regha‘*, 'moment', or *keregha‘*, 'as a moment', which in prophecy and poetry sometimes denotes 'suddenly'. How the noun comes to denote 'moment' is not our concern, but we shall mention, and criticize, the prevalent view at the end of this essay.[1] From 'moment' to 'suddenly' is an easy transition, considering the swiftness of the sudden event: it takes you unawares, it comes like a thunderclap, 'in a moment'. Anyhow, whenever used in this sense, like the other two words, *regha‘* has regard to disaster.

In Deutero-Isaiah, in the section announcing Babylon's defeat, two verses before that quoted above as containing *pith'om*,[2] we find *regha‘* in the same sense: 'And these two things shall come to thee in a moment in one day, the loss of children and widowhood, they shall come upon thee in their perfection'.[3] Jeremiah has *regha‘* in the same line as *pith'om*: 'Suddenly my tents are spoiled and my curtains in a moment'.[4] The Psalmist prays: 'Let all mine enemies be ashamed and confounded, let them return and be ashamed in a moment'.[5] As in numerous cases of *pith'om* and *petha‘*, the ruin 'in a moment' of one side will mean triumph to the other, but the immediate reference of the expression is to misfortune. Elihu, one of Job's friends, urges that high and low are equally at God's mercy: 'In a moment shall they die, and at midnight shall the people be troubled'.[6] Here there is no victorious party, unless it be God.

In several texts it is doubtful whether the sense is 'suddenly' or, less frightening, 'quickly', 'in an instant'. The Handwörterbuch favours the former—and we incline to agree—but Koehler the latter.[7] In Numbers, twice God tells Moses and Aaron to leave a guilty community 'and I shall consume them in a moment'.[8] Of the wicked, the Psalmist says: 'How are they become a desolation in a moment'.[9] In Lamentations we read: 'The iniquity of

---

[1] See below, pp. 78f..
[2] See p. 4.
[3] Is 47.9.
[4] Jer 4.20; see above, p. 4.
[5] Ps 6.11.
[6] Job 34.20.
[7] Gesenius' Handwörterbuch über das Alte Testament, 16th ed. by Buhl, 1915, 745, Koehler, Lexicon in Veteris Testamenti Libros, 1935, 874.
[8] Nu 16.21, 17.10.
[9] Ps 73.19.

the daughter of my people is greater than the sin of Sodom, that was overthrown in a moment'.[1]

In a passage from Exodus, the choice lies between 'suddenly' (Handwörterbuch) and 'for a short while' (Koehler), and it matters rather more than in the other cases. It is either 'Ye are a stiffnecked people, I will come up into the midst of thee in one moment and consume thee', or alternatively, 'If I came up into the midst of thee for one moment I would consume thee'.[2] The Handwörterbuch also brings under 'suddenly' a text from Sirach where, however, the meaning is plainly 'for a short while'. The section depicts the woes of man, leaving him no peace even at night: 'For a little, vainly, for a moment, he reposeth, and then is disturbed by dreams'.[3]

The verb *hirgia'* may signify 'to act suddenly' in a line which occurs twice in Jeremiah.[4] 'I will suddenly make him run away from her'. In Proverbs we read: 'The lip of truth shall be established for ever, and a lying tongue'—and now we may render 'as long as I give rest', 'for a moment', or 'until I act suddenly'.[5] Finally, a prophecy of Deutero-Isaiah: 'I will make my judgment to rest for a light of the people; my righteousness is near'.[6] On the basis of minor or major emendations of commentators, we might obtain 'in a short time my righteousness shall approach' or 'suddenly I bring near my righteousness'. If the latter interpretation is chosen, the prophet would here be stressing the menace of the judgment. But the text is too obscure to count.

3. ASSOCIATED WORDS

Looking back over the texts with 'suddenly', we notice that characteristic notions are apt to recur in them or their immediate neighbourhood. The 'sudden' event is 'an evil',[7] 'death',[8] 'blow',

---

[1] Lam 4.6.
[2] Ex 33.5.
[3] Si 40.6; text not intact, but general drift clear. For a similar mistranslation of *hereph 'ayin* by Strack-Billerbeck, see below, p. 77, footnote 6.
[4] Jer 49.19, 50.44; Rudolph, Jeremia, 1947, 248, 264, assumes a corruption.
[5] Pr 12.19.
[6] Is 51.4f.
[7] Is 47.11, Ec 9.12.
[8] Nu 6.9, 35.22f., Jo 10.9ff., Jer 18.21f., Job 9.23, 34.20.

'wound', 'smiting',[1] 'breaking',[2] 'desolation',[3] 'calamity',[4] 'fall',[5] 'spoiling',[6] 'consuming'.[7]

These things 'come' or 'come upon a man',[8] or 'fall upon a man'[9] or 'among men'.[10] Even in the law concerning the unwitting homicide, one of the cases listed is where he accidentally 'causes a stone to fall upon a man';[11] and the preposition 'on' is employed in the law requiring a Nazarite to bring a sacrifice 'if any man die very suddenly by him'—literally 'on him', *'alaw*.[12] (In English, 'on' may connote 'so as to cause trouble'; a landlady might say of her lodger that 'he fell sick, died, on me'.)

Man 'does not know' how these things happen.[13] They 'confuse' or 'terrorise' him.[14] 'Night' is their proper time.[15]

Needless to say, the Old Testament is full of sudden events, events thought of as sudden, though the term is not employed; the foregoing evidence is, therefore, very incomplete. Dinah's brothers 'came upon' her seducer and his fellow-citizens;[16] Gideon, encouraged by a Midianite's dream in which 'a cake came unto the Midianite tent and smote it and it fell', attacked the enemy at night;[17] the Psalmist prays, 'Let desolation come to my adversary, he shall not know, let him fall in it'[18]—these and numerous similar

---

[1] Jo 10.9f., 11.7f., Jer 18.21f., Ps 64.8.

[2] Is 30.13, Jer 4.20, 51.8, Pr 6.15, 29.1.

[3] *Sho'a* in Is 47.11, Pr 3.25, *mashshu'a* and *shamma* in Ps 73.18f.

[4] Pr 6.15, 24.22,

[5] Jer 51.8, Ps 73.18f.

[6] Jer 4.20, 6.26, 15.8.

[7] Ex 33.5, Nu 16.21, 17.10, Job 9.22f.

[8] Jo 10.9, 11.7, Is 47.9, 11, 48.3, Jer 6.26, 15.8, 18.22, Mal 3.1, Pr 3.25, 6.15.

[9] Is 47.11, Jer 15.8, Ec 9.12.

[10] Jo 11.7.

[11] Nu 35.22.

[12] Nu 6.9.

[13] Is 47.11, Pr 24.22, Ec 9.12. Absence of knowledge is implied also in Nu 35.22; cp. the description of the unwitting homicide as acting 'without knowledge' in Dt 4.42. This is not to deny the significance of the fact that Nu 35 does not actually use the root 'to know'—we cannot go into it here.

[14] The root *hmm* in Jo 10.9f., *bhl* in Jer 15.8, Ps 6.11, Job 22.10, *blh* Ps 73.19, *phd* Ps 64.2, Job 22.10, Pr 3.25.

[15] Jo 10.9, Job 34.20. In Is 29.5, about Sennacherib's discomfiture, this is not stated, but the reader is surely expected to remember the details: cp. Is 17.14, 37.36, II Ki 19.35.

[16] Gen 34.25, 27.

[17] Jud 7.13ff.

[18] Ps 35.8; cp. e.g. Is 47.11.

texts contemplate sudden disasters. The author, that is, had he been so minded, might well have used *pith'om, petha'* or *regha'*. There are many more cases, however, which, though well within our modern, large concept of 'sudden', would not at the time have fallen under any of those terms. In establishing their scope, it is safest to base on those texts where they are actually found.

4. THE LXX

a) *Renderings of pith'om, petha' and regha'*

The LXX makes no demonstrable difference between *pith'om, petha'* and *regha'*. (We consider, of course, only texts where *regha'* means 'suddenly'.[1]) *Pith'om* is translated *aphno*,[2] *exaisios*,[3] *exaiphnes* or *exapines*,[4] *eperchesthai*,[5] *eutheos*,[6] *parachrema*.[7] In three texts the LXX reads a form of *patha* or *pethi*, 'simple', 'foolish', instead of the Massoretic *pith'om*; it is certainly right about one of them—concerning a young man going after a woman—where it has *kepphousthai*, 'cajoled', 'ensnared'. [8] In the others, it translates *nepios*, 'fool',[9] and *parabainon*, 'transgressor'.[10] *Petha'* is translated *exaiphnes* or *exapines*,[11] *parachrema*,[12] *stigme*,[13] *dia tachous*.[14] *Regha'* is translated *eisapax*,[15] *aphno*,[16] *exaiphnes* or *exapines*,[17] *spoude*,[18]

---

[1] Hence not, e.g., Is 54.8, where it means 'for a moment', though see on this text below, p. 76.

[2] Jo 10.9, Jer 4.20 (where *regha'* may be included), 18.22, 51.8, Ec 9.12.

[3] Job 9.23, 22.10.

[4] Jo 11.7, Is 47.11, 48.3, Jer 6.26, 15.8, Mal 3.1, Ps 64.5, Pr 6.15 (where *petha'* may be included), 24.22, II Chr 29.36, Si 5.7, 11.21.

[5] Pr 3.25.

[6] Job 5.3.

[7] Nu 6.9, 12.4, Is 29.5, 30.13 (where *petha'* is included).

[8] Pr 7.22; see above, p. 6.

[9] Ps 64.8.

[10] Si 40.14. This case is not clear; see Box and Oesterley, op. cit., 462. In Si 21.22, as argued above, p. 8, the Hebrew original had *mehera*, not *pith'om*: LXX *tachys*.

[11] Nu 6.9, 35.22, Hab 2.7, Pr 6.15 (possibly—see above, footnote 4, in connection with *pith'om*), 29.1.

[12] Is 30.13; see above, footnote 7, in connection with *pith'om*.

[13] Is 29.5.

[14] Si 11.21.

[15] Nu 16.21, 17.10.

[16] Jer 4.20 (possibly—see above, footnote 2, in connection with *pith'om*).

[17] Is 47.9, Ps 73.19.

[18] Lam 4.6.

dia tachous;[1] and the verb *hirgia'* appears as *tachys*.[2] In one text *regha'* is not rendered at all,[3] in another the LXX reads *negha'*, 'plague', and translates *plege*.[4]

Presumably much of the variety is due to laxness or different hands, though in some cases one can think of a reason for the stronger expression—*aphno, exaisios, exaiphnes*—or the less frightening one—*eisapax, eutheos, parachrema, spoude, stigme, tachys*. In a passage from Proverbs, *eperchesthai*, 'to come', which we mentioned above as typically associated with 'suddenly', actually does service for the latter. 'Be not afraid of sudden terror' in Hebrew, LXX 'Be not afraid of terror that cometh'.[5] Similarly, a variant in a passage from Numbers brings in 'lack of knowledge', also, we saw, often coupled with 'suddenly'. 'If any man die very suddenly by him' is explained as *agnoountos*, 'without his knowing'.[6]

Contrary to the prevalent myth, Aquila is not much tidier than the LXX. In the Hexapla we find noted: *arthroos,*[7] *aphno,*[8] *exaiphnes,*[9] *parachrema*.[10] Symmachus has *aphno,*[11] *aiphnidios,*[12] *exaiphnes*.[13]

b) *Related texts*

A few words about the remaining use by the LXX of these words, or some of them at least, may be in place.

Aphno recurs in Proverbs where the Hebrew says 'when your terror cometh as a desolation'.[14] Note the characteristic words 'terror', 'desolation', 'to come'.[15] In Ecclesiastes, however, in a variant, *aphno* describes the abruptness of a fool. 'When the fool

---

[1] Ps 6.11.
[2] Is 51.4f., Jer 49.19, 50.44, Pr 12.19.
[3] Job 34.20.
[4] Ex 33.5.
[5] Pr 3.25.
[6] Nu 6.9.
[7] Ps 6.11; but conceivably his rendering here is *exaiphnes*.
[8] Jer 15.8.
[9] Is 29.5, and maybe Ps 6.11.
[10] Ps 64.5, 8, Pr 6.15, 7.22, Job 5.3.
[11] Pr 6.15, Job 9.23.
[12] Ps 64.8.
[13] Jer 49.19, Ps 6.11, Pr 7.22, Job 22.10, Lam 4.6.
[14] Pr 1.27.
[15] 'Terror', *pahadh*, 'desolation', *sho'a*. Further on in the same verse 'calamity', 'to come upon a man'.

walketh' in Hebrew, a variant of the LXX 'when he walketh suddenly'.[1]

In I Maccabees, the word is employed, as in Joshua, of the surprise assault of an army—with 'to leap upon', 'fall', 'to fall upon', 'smiting', 'night', 'to kill'.[2] In II Maccabees, Heliodorus, about to violate the Temple, is visited by a fearful apparition and 'suddenly' drops to the ground; he is enwrapped by 'darkness'.[3]

Symmachus has *aphno* in Psalms. Hebrew 'For it passeth quickly and we fly away'; Symmachus 'For suddenly cut off we fly away'.[4]

A survey of *aphno* must be supplemented by *aiphnidios*. In Wisdom, during the plague of darkness the Egyptians are haunted by apparitions and 'sudden fear came upon them'—with typical words and setting.[5] In Maccabees we hear three times of a 'sudden' military attack;[6] also of an army thrown into 'sudden consternation'.[7]

Symmachus translates *regha'* by *aiphnidios* in Ezekiel's prophecy against Tyrus: the princes of the sea will tremble 'at the sudden things'—Hebrew 'every moment'.[8] Note 'fall', 'slaughter', 'desolation', 'terror' in this section.[9] That he uses *aiphnidios* for the 'sudden' arrow in Psalms we mentioned above.[10] Another case in Psalms is interesting. The Massoretic text offers two versions, 'May desolation be upon them (my persecutors)' or 'May death seize upon them'.[11] Symmachus has: 'May sudden death come upon them'. It looks as if he had wished to do justice to both alternatives.

Next, *exaisios*. Several texts in Job. In the first, the Hebrew runs 'mine ear received a whisper (?) from him', and the LXX has *exaisia*, 'terrible things', for 'whisper'.[12] The Hebrew consonants

---

[1] Ec 10.3; the principal reading is *aphron*. As for the 'suddenness' of a fool, cp. above, p. 6, in connection with Pr 7.22, and below, pp. 15f., 24f., in connection with Lev 21.4, Nu 4.20, and the Rabbinic discussions regarding the sudden entry of a house.

[2] I Mac 3.23, 4.2, 5.28; cp. Jo 10.9.

[3] II Mac 3.27.

[4] Ps 90.10.

[5] Wi 17.15; cp. below, p. 17, on Wi 18.17, in connection with *parachrema*.

[6] II Mac 5.5, 14.22, III Mac 3.24.

[7] II Mac 14.17.

[8] Ez 26.16.

[9] 'Desolation', *shmm*, 'terror', *bhl*.

[10] Ps 64.8; see p. 13.

[11] Ps 55.16. The former is 'what is written', the latter 'what is to be read'. The word for 'desolation' is related with *shmm*.

[12] Job 4.12.

are *shmṣ*; maybe the LXX reads a form of *shmm*, 'desolation', one
of the words often accompanying 'suddenly'. In the following two
verses we find 'night' and 'terror'.[1] Then we meet *exaisios* as an
attribute of 'calamity', with no equivalent in the Hebrew.[2] 'Terror'
and 'death' in the same section.[3] In another passage, in the Hebrew
'the joy of the wicked is short', in the LXX it is 'a terrible ruin'.[4]
Probably the LXX does mean to translate the Hebrew before us,
stressing the quick end.

Three times *exaisios* stands for the root *pl'*, 'wondrous', 'awesome',[5] and a fourth time it has this meaning without an equivalent
in the Hebrew.[6] In these cases there is no allusion to disaster.
Yet the 'wondrous', even when beneficial, surpasses comfortable
understanding, is uncanny, not easy to rely on, to live with. We
shall come back to this aspect in the section on the New Testament,
where 'suddenly', though no longer confined to disaster, is confined
to the sphere of the 'wondrous'; *exaisios* does not occur.

In Habakkuk, a variant twice has *exaisios* as an attribute of a
thunderstorm or waters stirred up by the coming of God:[7] no
equivalent in the Hebrew text. Plainly another instance of the
sense 'wondrous'.

Exaiphnes or *exapines* occurs in a Pentateuchic section forbidding
a priest to defile himself for any dead except his nearest relations.
The Hebrew goes on: 'He shall not defile himself, a master among
his people'.[8] The LXX reads *balla'* for *ba'al*, thus obtaining 'suddenly' in the place of 'a master'. The word, however, approaches
here the meaning 'thoughtlessly', 'without due consideration'. In
another section we are informed of the arrangements needed before
the Kohathites may approach the holiest of holies. The Hebrew
goes on: 'And they shall not come to see the sanctuary *kebhalla'*,
for a moment'.[9] The LXX translates again 'suddenly', i.e. 'thoughtlessly', 'without the prescribed arrangements'. Below, we shall
adduce a Midrash dealing with a provision in Leviticus which

---

[1] Job 4.13f.; 'terror', *paḥadh*.
[2] Job 18.12.
[3] Job 18.11, 13f.
[4] Job 20.5.
[5] Job 5.9, 9.10, 37.16.
[6] Job 34.24.
[7] Hab 3.10, 15.
[8] Lev 21.4; text hardly intact.
[9] Nu 4.20; translation dubious.

debars Aaron from free, informal access to the sanctuary: it is in
the course of this discussion that the Midrash quotes Rabbinic
utterances against entering a house 'suddenly', *pith'om*.[1] There
may or may not be a connection between this kind of 'suddenness',
'thoughtlessness', and the 'suddenness' of the fool we touched on
in discussing the young man seduced from Proverbs.[2]

Micah threatens the wicked: 'And ye shall not walk upright'.[3]
The LXX adds 'suddenly'. The word 'evil' occurs in this verse,
'spoiling' in the next. Daniel repeatedly speaks of a conqueror who
succeeds 'in security'.[4] Apparently he exploits his victim's feeling
of security. At any rate, while Theodotion translates en *eutheniai*,
the LXX substitutes *exapina*. The associated words 'to come' and
'breaking' occur in these verses.[5]

To Sirach's condemnation of corrupt children a variant adds that
their end will take place 'suddenly'.[6] We must, however, recall
another passage, where 'suddenly' refers to the bestowal of riches
on a good, pious man.[7] As observed above, we suspect that the
Hebrew original was different. At least in the Greek, *exapina* has
completely lost its sinister overtones, though, conceivably, the
author may mean to convey the element of the 'wondrous'.

In I Maccabees, as in Joshua, the word signifies the surprise
assault of an army.[8] Note 'to fall upon', 'smite', 'destroy', 'blow'.
In III Maccabees we find destruction 'suddenly' decreed against
the Jews.[9]

Symmachus, where the Psalmist says 'I would hasten my escape',
puts 'Suddenly I would make my escape'.[10]

Parachrema means 'straightway', 'forthwith', in II Samuel.
The Hebrew reads 'Abner sent messengers on his behalf'.[11] The
expression 'on his behalf', *tahtaw*, literally 'under himself', 'for

---

[1] Lev Rabba on 16.2f.
[2] Pr 7.22; see above, p. 6.
[3] Mi 2.3.
[4] Dan 11.21, 24.
[5] 'To come' in Dan 11.21, 24, 'breaking' in 24. In the latter verse the LXX
substitutes 'he shall lay waste' for 'he shall come'; altogether the LXX aims
at clarification of the somewhat dark original.
[6] Si 13.3.
[7] Si 11.21; see above, p. 8.
[8] I Mac 1.30; cp. Jo 11.7.
[9] III Mac 4.2.
[10] Ps 55.9.
[11] II Sam 3.12; text possibly corrupt, translation dubious.

himself', occasionally signifies 'at his place'.[1] The LXX—as also Theodotion—is proceeding from this usage when it puts 'straightway': we may compare 'on the spot', *auf der Stelle* or, slightly less close, *sur-le-champ*. Similarly, in Job, 'Tread down the wicked *taḥtam*, where they stand',[2] in the LXX leads to *parachrema*, 'straightway'; and an obscure clause in Psalms, something like 'and he was exalted *taḥath*, under, my tongue',[3] is rendered by Symmachus 'and straightway my tongue was exalted'.

In two passages *parachrema*, though probably denoting 'straightway', has definite ties with 'suddenly'. The Psalmist asks help against his enemies: 'May they be desolate as a reward for their shame'.[4] Rendered by the LXX: 'May they get as reward *parachrema* their shame'. The reference to 'desolation', so often associated with 'suddenly',[5] accounts for this interpretation. This is confirmed by the other case, from Job. Hebrew: 'The young ones of the eagle suck up blood, and where the slain are, there is he'.[6] The Hebrew for 'there' is *sham*, which the LXX takes as a form of 'desolation'—hence translating 'and where the slain are, *parachrema* they are found'.

The particle signifies 'suddenly' in Wisdom, in a description of the overthrow of the Egyptians: 'Then suddenly apparitions in terrible dreams troubled them'—with characteristic associated terms and in nocturnal setting.[7] In Maccabees, on the other hand, it invariably means 'straightway': 'and straightway he despatched him',[8] 'straightway he stripped off Andronicus's purple robe',[9] 'had he pressed forward, he would straightway have been turned back',[10] 'the king commanded to heat the pans, and these were straightway heated',[11] 'he straightway took possession',[12] 'send someone straight-

---

[1] E.g. II Sam 2.23, 'he died in the same place'; LXX *hypokato autou*.
[2] Job 40.12.
[3] Ps 66.17.
[4] Ps 40.16.
[5] The root used in Ps 40.16 is *shmm*.
[6] Job 39.20.
[7] Wi 18.17; cp. 17.15 quoted above, p. 14, for *aiphnidios*.
[8] II Mac 4.34.
[9] II Mac 4.38.
[10] II Mac 5.18.
[11] II Mac 7.4.
[12] II Mac 10.22.

way',[1] and finally, the martyrs bravely faced threats to be executed 'straightway'.[2]

In Tobith, according to the Codex Sinaiticus, Raphael went after the demon and 'bound him straightway'.[3] The Vaticanus and Alexandrinus do not have the adverb. Either the Sinaiticus has added it, in order to make the deed even more splendid, or its absence from the other recension is due to abbreviation.[4] Comparable divergences in Bel and the Dragon. According to the LXX Habakkuk was miraculously brought back from Babylon to Palestine 'on the same day', according to Theodotion 'straightway';[5] and Daniel's enemies, thrown into the den, 'were devoured' according to the LXX, 'were devoured straightway' according to Theodotion.[6]

Symmachus in Psalms seems to use *parachrema* in the sense of 'suddenly'. Hebrew: 'Our steps have now compassed me'.[7] Symmachus reads *'ishsheruni*, 'they praise me happy', for *'ashshurenu*, 'our steps', and renders: 'While praising me happy, suddenly they (the wicked ones) compassed me'.

We might add that a Greek and, indeed, a Hebrew 'suddenly' is to be assumed behind *subito expavescent* in IV Ezra[8]—the last trumpet striking people with fear. It would be idle to try and be specific as to which of the foregoing terms would be the most likely.

Eperchesthai is too common to be presented in detail. It may suffice to point out that it is practically confined to adverse and 'wondrous' things—on which latter we remarked in connection with *exaisios*.

Euthys, on the other hand, is truly neutral; and so is *tachys* which usually corresponds to the Hebrew root *mhr*, 'speed', 'haste'. *Stigme* recurs in II Maccabees, where we are told how the pains of Antiochus Epiphanes increased *kata stigmen*, 'from moment to moment'.,

Spoude[9] with which we take *spoudazein*, at first sight neutral,

---

[1] II Mac 11.36.
[2] IV Mac 14.9.
[3] To 8.3.
[4] The latter solution would fit in with the evaluation of Simpson, in Charles, op. cit., vol. 1, 175f.
[5] Bel 39.
[6] Bel 42.
[7] Ps 17.11; text hardly intact.
[8] IV Ezra 6.23.
[9] II Mac 9.11; the intactness of the text has been questioned.

is more often than not associated with disagreeableness. Haste is
pleasant when you are making for a joyful occasion. It is unpleasant
when you are fleeing a disaster, and also when you are being driven,
hurried. The two kinds of unpleasantness may merge: Lot was
'hurried' by the angels in order that he should escape the ruin of
Sodom,[1] and in a way the departure of the Israelites from Egypt
belongs here—they were 'hurried' by their oppressors who were
afraid that the slaughter of the firstborn might become a universal
one.[2] Deutero-Isaiah proclaims that, by contrast, the forthcoming
second exodus will not be 'with hurry (scare, anxious flight)'.[3] In
the LXX *spoude* and *spoudazein* are in the main unpleasant.

They are so in most texts where the underlying Hebrew is *bhl*,
'confusion', 'terror', a root referred to above as among those characteristically adjoining suddenness.[4] Two of the texts in question
actually do contain *pith'om*.[5] Again, there is one text where the
underlying Hebrew is *hmm*, 'confusion', another root often accompanying suddenness;[6] one text, just mentioned, about Lot, where
the Hebrew is *'uṣ*, 'to hurry on';[7] three texts, just mentioned,
about the departure from Egypt, in two of which the Hebrew
is *ḥippazon*, 'hurry', 'scare', 'anxious flight', represented by *bhl*
in the Targum,[8] in the third *miher*, 'to hurry on';[9] one text where the
Hebrew is *b'ṭ*, 'terror', a root sometimes alleged to be related to
petha', 'suddenly';[10] and finally, one text where the Hebrew is

---

[1] Gen 19.15.

[2] Ex 12.33.

[3] Is 52.12, *ḥippazon*, cp. Ex 12.11, Dt 16.3. The LXX translates *tarache*
in Is, *spoude* in Ex and Dt: we shall presently encounter a similar difference
between Jer 14.19 and 8.15.

[4] See p. 11.

[5] Jer 15.8, Job 22.10. The others are: Is 21.5, Zeph 1.18, Ps 78.33,
Job 4.5, 21.6, 23.15f., Dan 2.25 (hurry to prevent a disaster; Theodotion
has *spoude* also in 3.24, 6.20, in both cases hurry in discomfort). Towards the
end of this essay, below, p. 73, we shall touch on *bhl* as denoting 'speed' in
the service of a king. The LXX has *spoude*, *spoudazein*, *speudo* and *epispeudo*:
Ec 8.3, Esth 2.9, 6.14, 8.14, Ezra 4.23, I Esdras 2.30 (cp. 6.10). In I
Sam 21.9 it has *kata spouden* for the king's business which was *naḥuṣ*,
'pressed', 'pressing'.

[6] Ez 7.11. The Hebrew text is obscure and hardly intact.

[7] Gen 19.15.

[8] Ex 12.11, Dt 16.3.

[9] Ex 12.33.

[10] Jer 8.15; see above, p. 3. In 14.19 the same Hebrew is rendered *tarache*,
'trouble', 'confusion': cp. above, footnote 3, concerning the difference between
Ex 12.11 and Dt 16.3 on the one hand, Is 52.12 on the other.

regha', 'moment', 'suddenly'.[1] In some passages where it is difficult to say exactly which Hebrew word *spoude* is intended to
render, we can at least note that it qualifies fearful happenings.[2]

In the Apocrypha, little remains of this Septuagintal colouring
of *spoude*. Occasionally an old tradition comes through. Wisdom of
Solomon, explaining the origins of idolatry, remarks on the desire
of princes to receive homage even from subjects living afar; these
had to make images of the princes, 'that by their zeal they might
flatter the absent (princes) as if they were present'.[3] Here *spoude*
means 'zeal', 'diligence', 'striving'—as usually in Hellenistic wri-
tings.[4] By contrast, in the description of how the Egyptians
'pressed the Israelites to be gone and sent them forth with speed',
the unpleasant sense of 'driving', 'hurrying on', present in the exodus account of the LXX,[5] is adopted.

5. THE TARGUM

To turn to the Targum—here we do find a difference made
between *pith'om* and *petha'* on the one hand and *regha'* on the other.
The usual rendering of the former two is *bithekheph*.[6]

In Proverbs *shilya'* is favoured to render 'suddenly'.[7] Significantly, the word—as a feminine noun—may stand for 'desolation'.[8]
In one passage, where the Hebrew says that the obdurate sinner
'shall suddenly be broken', the Targum has *ba'aghala'*, 'with speed'.[9]
The young man following the seductress does so *sheli'ayith*.[10] This
may well mean the same as *shilya'*; it is simply an adverbial form.
It is, however, conceivable that, by the slight change from the
usual, the translator is indicating that we ought to bear in mind

---

[1] Lam 4.6; see pp. 9f., 12.

[2] Panicky flight in Jud 5.22, Dan 10.7; punishments and fears of the
wicked in Theodotion's version of Dan 9.27, 11.44.

[3] Wi 14.17.

[4] No need to assume a direct link with *bhl* and *spoude* in the specific sense
of 'haste in the service of a king' to be mentioned below, p. 73; the relevant
texts are already quoted above, p. 19, footnote 5.

[5] Ex 12.33, see above, p. 19.

[6] Nu 6.9, 12.4, 35.22, Jo 10.9, 11.7, Is 29.5, 30.13, 47.11, 48.3, Jer
4.20, 6.26, 15.8, 18.22, 51.8, Hab 2.7, Mal 3.1, Ps 64.5, 8, Job 5.3, 9.23,
22.10.

[7] Pr 3.25, 6.15 (for *pith'om* and for *petha'*), 24.22.

[8] E.g. Ps 35.8, Hebrew *sho'a*.

[9] Pr 29.1.

[10] Pr 7.22.

another application of the root, namely, 'security', 'thoughtlessness'[1]. As already remarked, the Hebrew must originally have had to do with *patha* or *pethi*, 'simple', 'foolish', and the LXX translates *kepphousthai*.

In Ecclesiastes, instead of 'when evil time falleth suddenly upon them', we get 'when evil time falleth upon them *righ'a' hadha' mishshemayya'*, in one moment from heaven'.[2] It is strange that this is the only occurrence in the Targum of *righ'a'*, etymologically identical with Hebrew *regha'*; yet it is *pith'om*, not *regha'*, which is being thus translated.

Regha' in the texts considered above is represented by *sha'a'*, 'a short time', 'a moment',[3] *zeman*, 'time', 'moment',[4] or *zeman hadha'*, 'one moment';[5] the verb *hirgia'* by *zeman*, 'moment',[6] or *'istarhebh*, 'hasty'.[7]

6. THE DEAD SEA SCROLLS

In the Dead Sea Scrolls, in Habakkuk, *pith'om* replaces the Massoretic *petha'*: no change in sense, it is just a substitution of the commoner term.[8] As will presently be observed,[9] *petha'* is extremely rare in Rabbinic literature.

Pith'om recurs in the Zadokite Fragments.[10] The text, which is corrupt,[11] may refer to the wicked being 'suddenly' punished; though most authorities emend into *petha'im* so as to obtain punishment of the 'foolish', as in a line which occurs twice in Proverbs.[12] Above we discussed another case in Proverbs where *pith'om* may be substituted for an original *petha'im*.[13] The line here in question indeed means that 'the foolish (imprudent) pass on (when evil threatens) and are made to pay for it', while the Zadokite Frag-

---

[1] Cp. II Sam 3.27.
[2] Ec 9.12.
[3] Ex 33.5, Nu 16.21, 17.10, Ps 6.11, 73.19, Job 34.20, Lam 4.6.
[4] Is 47.9.
[5] Jer 4.20.
[6] Jer 49.19, 50.44.
[7] Pr 12.19.
[8] Hab 2.7; 8.13 in the Scroll.
[9] See p. 22.
[10] Zad Fr 14.2.
[11] Though see now Kuhn, Revue de Qumran 14, 1963, 220 n. 164a.
[12] Pr 22.3, 27.12. The prevalent spelling in 22.3 is *pethayim*, in 27.12 *petha'yim* (with an aleph), so the latter is closer to *pith'om*.
[13] Pr 7.22; see pp. 5f.

ments mean, 'the foolish (wicked, blind) transgress and are punished. But this re-interpretation is found also among the Rabbis.[1] Actually, we shall see that they somehow associate *pith'om* with it: so there may, after all, be a case for not altering the word in the Fragments and yet accepting that they speak of the punishment of the 'foolish'.

Two passages from the Hymns. One, while extremely fragmentary, may confidently be regarded as dealing with the judgment on the wicked.[2] The other at first sight speaks of a blessing: 'Suddenly the waters shall gush forth which were hidden in secret'. But on closer examination these turn out to be the waters of curse for the damned; and the very use of *pith'om* supports this interpretation—the author is thinking of the judgment.[3]

Regha' in the sense of 'suddenly' is not evidenced in the Dead Sea Scrolls. Indeed there is so far only one defective place where the root may possibly be employed.[4]

7. TALMUD AND MIDRASH

In Talmud and Midrash, in general, *pith'om* still refers to the terrifying or at least the unwelcome. But only in general: it can now also describe happy occurrences. *Petha'* is hardly used — the Habakkuk Scroll, we saw, turns it into *pith'om*[5] — *regha'* in the sense of 'suddenly' not at all. The disappearance of *regha'* is easily accounted for: even the Old Testament never uses it for 'suddenly' in prose.

In Mishnah and Tosephta, *pith'om* and *petha'* are not met—hardly surprising in view of the legal character of these collections. It is true that the words occur in two provisions in Numbers, cited above.[6] But by Talmudic times the qualification expressed by them was subsumed under, swallowed up by, wider technical terms such as *sheghagha*, 'error', 'inadvertence', now the standard characterization of unwitting homicide.[7]

---

[1] Bab. Keritoth 9a, Nu Rabba on 6.9; see below, p. 26.
[2] Hymns 17.5; see Licht, The Thanksgiving Scrolls, 1957, 206f.
[3] Hymns 8.18; cp. Licht, op. cit., 136.
[4] War Rule 5.18.
[5] Above, p. 21.
[6] Nu 6.9, 35.22; see p. 3.
[7] E.g. Mishnah Makkoth 2.1. As for the Rabbinic treatment of Nu 6.9, see below, pp. 25f.

Johanan ben Zaccai, 1st century A.D., compares the end to a meal to which a king invited his servants without fixing a date. Whether the Rabbi has in mind death, or the day of the Lord, or both, is dubious. The probability is that this kind of parable was common in eschatological discourse, where it alluded to the day of the Lord; and that ben Zaccai is thinking primarily of individual death, i.e. he somewhat changes the application of the simile. Anyhow the foolish servants went about their business, convinced that no meal could start without preparation. They fared badly when the king 'suddenly' summoned his guests[1]. We found this usage in the Old Testament: the 'sudden' judgment to be feared.[2]

However, we also noticed that frequently what is calamity for one side is triumph for the other. Even the judgment will end in purification and bliss for the righteous. How 'suddenly' may acquire a different connotation when the emphasis shifts over to the positive aspect of an event is exemplified by Malachi's prophecy, quoted above: 'Behold, I send my messenger and he shall prepare the way before me, and the Lord shall suddenly come to his temple'.[3] In the original, a threat. But in a Midrashic discussion of the faithless spies sent out by Moses to explore Canaan, it has become a merely comforting promise: 'In this world, as they were messengers of mortals, they did not enter the land; but in the World to Come I send you my messenger suddenly and he (i.e. a messenger, not of mortals, but of God) will prepare the way, as predicted by Malachi'.[4] An alternative translation would be 'they were mortal messengers', in which case 'my messenger' must be conceived of as a supernatural being, an angel or the like. It makes no difference to our argument.

Perhaps we should also note that while in the original text the coming of the Lord is sudden, in the Midrash it is the preparatory sending of the messenger. Two possible explanations. Either, for the Midrash, 'the messenger' and 'the lord' are identical. That is to say, the two clauses 'I send my messenger' and 'the lord will come' are regarded as saying more or less the same. Which leads to the interpretation 'I send my messenger suddenly', 'the messenger—the lord—will come suddenly'. Or the 'suddenly' is deli-

---

[1] Bab. Shabbath 153a.
[2] Mal 3.1, to which we shall come back presently.
[3] Mal 3.1.
[4] Nu Rabba on 13.17.

berately—we might almost say, arbitrarily—transferred from the coming to the sending, on the strength perhaps of the exegetical method *seres*, in Greek *anastrophe*. The Midrash, that is, prefers to ascribe suddenness to the preparatory cleansing instead of to the subsequent theophany. Whichever explanation we choose, the Midrash's motive was to overcome an apparently serious difficulty in Malachi's formulation; namely, that after preparation by the messenger, the coming should none the less be sudden. The contradiction is seen by Powis Smith,[1] though the majority of modern commentators fail to notice it.[2] In a subsequent paragraph of this study we shall say something on there being room for the sudden within the expected, provided the latter is sufficiently general.[3]

An instance of typical Rabbinic use of *pith'om* is provided by Akiba's maxim (first half of 2nd century A.D.): 'Do not enter your house suddenly, still less another man's'.[4] It was adopted by his disciple Simeon ben Johai.[5] In the Midrash, the latter's version is ingeniously, though no doubt secondarily, given as a comment on the law in Leviticus that Aaron may enter the sanctuary only with much formality—properly attired and offering the prescribed sacrifice: 'he may not enter at all times'.[6] It may be recalled that the LXX uses *exapina* in a similar provision in Numbers (concerning the Kohathites' approach to the sanctuary), where the Hebrew has not got 'suddenly'.[7]

The same section of the Midrash contains an anecdote about another disciple of Akiba's, Hananiah ben Hakinai. He came home 'suddenly' after an absence of thirteen years devoted to study. His wife's soul left her and returned only in answer to his prayer.

According to Johanan bar Nappaha, first half of 3rd century A.D., Sirach condemns him 'who enters another man's house suddenly'; the Rabbi adds that one's own house should be included.[8] As observed above, Sirach himself here used, not *pith'om*, but the more neutral *mehera*, 'hastily'.[9] Rab, an older contemporary

---

[1] The Book of Malachi, 1912, 63.
[2] E.g. Horst, Die Zwölf Kleinen Propheten, 1938, 263.
[3] See below, pp. 74f.
[4] Bab. Pesahim 112a.
[5] Bab. Nidda 16b, Lev Rabba on 16.2f.
[6] Lev 16.2f.
[7] Nu 4.20; see above, pp. 15f.
[8] Bab. Nidda 16b. We are told that he saw in Sirach's saying an interpretation of Pr 19.16, 'He who is careless of his ways shall die'.
[9] Si 21.22; Greek *tachys*. See above, pp. 8, 12, footnote 10.

of bar Nappaha's, supplies an extension of the usual warning:
'Do not enter into a city suddenly'—quite possibly directed
against surprise official inspections.[1] The maxim may indeed ante-
date Rab.[2]

In Derek Eres we are told that the proper conduct of not entering
another's home 'suddenly' may be learnt from God's example.
When he 'called unto Adam, where art thou?' he must have stood
at the door of the garden: he announced himself before entering.[3]

The Rabbinic discussion of the requirement in Numbers that a
Nazarite must bring a sacrifice 'if any man die very suddenly by
him'[4] involves several artificial interpretations of *pith'om* and *petha'*.
But even these are evidence that by now the words are less uncom-
promisingly sinister.

The Biblical text has the double phrase *bephetha' pith'om*. The
Siphre holds[5] that the requirement is thereby extended beyond
intentional defilement: *petha'* includes constraint, *pith'om* inadvertence, or vice versa—the former alternative seems to be advocated
by Josiah, the latter is advocated by Jonathan. Both were disciples
of Ishmael, around the middle of the 2nd century A.D.

According to Numbers Rabba,[6] Jonathan rests his interpretation
of *petha'* as inadvertence on the law concerning the unwitting
homicide, where the word has this sense,[7] that of *pith'om* as constraint on the presence of the word in God's summons, 'And God
spake suddenly to Moses, Aaron and Miriam'.[8]

Kuhn suggests that Jonathan did not in fact make use of these
texts.[9] But this may be hypercritical. That the texts may not
appear sound arguments to us moderns is neither here nor there.
It should be noted that they are the only ones in the Pentateuch
in which *petha'* and *pith'om* recur again. That is to say, as far as
the Pentateuch is concerned, we have to do with *dis legomena*—the
importance of which class in early Rabbinic exegesis has been

---

[1] Jastrow, A Dictionary of the Targumim, the Talmud and Midrashic
Literature, 1926, 1250.
[2] See Bacher, Die Agada der Tannaiten, vol. 1, 2nd ed., 1903, 270f.
[3] Gen 3.9, Derek Eres Rabba 5.
[4] Nu 6.9.
[5] Siphre on Nu 6.9.
[6] Nu Rabba on 6.9.
[7] Nu 35.22; see above, p. 3.
[8] Nu 12.4; see above, p. 3.
[9] Sifre zu Numeri, 1933, 97.

established by Schwarz even though one may not follow him all the way[1]. Our thesis is not affected by the question.

The notion of God's summons as 'constraint', *'ones*, is very interesting. It, or something very like it, recurs at least in one more post-Biblical text; namely, in the Passover Hagadah, in an early exposition of a portion of Deuteronomy—more precisely, of the clause 'and he (Jacob) went down into Egypt'.[2] Perhaps the author of the exposition vocalized *wayyuradh*, 'and he was brought down', instead of *wayyeredh*, 'and he went down'. Anyhow Jacob, he tells us, was 'constrained, *'anus*, by the Word': doubtless he is thinking of the vision Jacob received on his way to Egypt at Beersheba.[3]

We also learn from Numbers Rabba that the interpretation— probably Josiah's—of *pith'om* as inadvertence may be based on Proverbs, 'The fool believeth every word'.[4] Obviously, *pith'om* is here treated as an adverb belonging to *patha, pethi*, 'foolish', 'simple'.[5] Unfortunately we are not informed what text might support *petha‘* as referring to constraint. A further possible understanding of *pith'om*, however, is added by the Rabbis at large; namely, as denoting the intentional deed. Proof is found in the passage from Proverbs, 'The fools (imprudent ones) pass on', to which the Rabbis (like the Zadokite Fragments mentioned above) ascribe the sense, 'The fools (wicked ones) transgress'.[6]

The subsequent exegesis of the Nazarite's obligation in this source proceeds from the assumption—clearly the one which prevailed— that, while *petha‘* designates inadvertence, *pith'om* may be used indiscriminately for intention, constraint or inadvertence.

The Talmudic comments on the matter look like summaries of those in Numbers Rabba. At any rate, they arrive at the same final conclusions.[7]

To repeat, what emerges is that, in Rabbinic usage, *pith'om* and *petha‘*, while no longer confined to adversity, still mostly qualify

---

[1] Die Hermeneutische Analogie in der Talmudischen Litteratur, 1897, 61ff.

[2] Dt 26.5, Die Pessach-Haggada, ed. Goldschmidt, 1936, 48.

[3] Gen 46.2ff.; *yaradh*, 'to go down', both in 46.3 and 4. It is Gen 46.2ff., incidentally, which Mt 2.13 is designed to parallel; see Daube, New Testament Studies 5, 1959, 184f.

[4] Pr 14.15.

[5] See above, pp. 5f., 12, 21f.

[6] Pr 22.3, 27.12, Zad Fr 14.2; see above, pp. 21f.

[7] Bab. Keritoth 9a, even shorter Jer. Nazir 57a.

happenings not of a joyful character. This is underlined by the almost regular absence of the terms where, otherwise, they might be expected. For example, 'Three come', a Tannaitic saying goes, 'when thoughts are elsewhere, the Messiah, a find and a scorpion'[1]. For R. Zera (beginning of the 4th century A.D.), who transmits the saying, it was indeed convenient that it had this formulation, instead of one with 'sudden'. He used it to discourage his colleagues from speculation about the date of redemption: such speculation (which, incidentally, was frowned on by many from early times) would delay redemption since their thoughts were not elsewhere.

The following case illustrates even better what, in overall effect, amounts to an avoidance of the terms on pleasant occasions—illustrates it better because, from our point of view, the terms would be so highly appropriate. R. Hiyya the Elder (about A.D. 200) thinks that redemption will begin like the dawn and only by stages attain its full splendour.[2] The reason, according to R. Judan (middle of the 4th century A.D.), is that Israel, deep in sorrows, could not bear deliverance 'all at once'; just as, if the sun wheeled up without being preceded by the dawn, the creatures would be blinded.[3] The Rabbis proceed from the experience that even sudden joy or sudden removal of pressure may do harm. But we find neither *pith'om* nor *petha'*. In Judan's statement we find *bebhath 'aḥath*, 'all at once', 'in one go' (*eisapax, auf ein Mal*).

---

[1] Bab. Sanhedrin 97a.
[2] Song of Solomon Rabba on 6.10, Esth Rabba on 8.15.
[3] Midrash Psalms on 18.51. Bacher, Die Agada der Palästinensischen Amoräer, vol. 3, 1899, 246, suggests that Judan's resumption of the old idea may have been prompted by Julian's relaxations.

CHAPTER TWO

THE NEW TESTAMENT

I. 'SUDDEN' AND 'SUDDENLY'

The following words are used in the New Testament for 'sudden' or 'suddenly': *aiphnidios, aphno, exaiphnes, exapina*. They may be described as rare. *Aiphnidios* occurs once in Luke, once in I Thessalonians; *aphno* only in Acts, three times; *exaiphnes* five times—once in Mark, twice in Luke, twice in Acts; *exapina* once, in Mark. To be sure, there is an occasional circumlocution[1]. But the general picture is not affected: the notion, we shall see, is confined to a very few areas.

Aiphnidios. 'Take heed', says Luke, 'lest that day come upon you as a sudden one, as a snare, for it shall come upon all them that dwell on earth'.[2] This is the traditional fear of the apocalyptic day, represented in the Old Testament, for example, by Malachi, quoted above,[3] and in Rabbinism by the parable of the summons to the feast—though ben Zaccai, we suggested, possibly reduces its application to the individual's death.[4] The appearence of 'to come upon' in this context is significant: from early on this verb is associated with sudden calamity.[5]

In the Marcan parallel the word employed is *exaiphnes*,[6] in Matthew this particular passage is not paralleled. However, both in Matthew and in Luke, in the parable of the servant put in authority, we find a close circumlocution. The arrival at the moment of reckoning, that is, is depicted in a way that might constitute a definition of 'suddenness': 'The lord shall come in a day when he looketh not and in an hour that he knoweth not'.[7] 'Not to know',

---

[1] See presently, at the foot of this page, on Mt 24.50, Lk 12.46.
[2] Lk 21.34f.
[3] Mal 3.1; see above, pp. 4f.
[4] Bab. Shabbath 153a; see above, p. 23.
[5] See above, p. 11. Lk 21.34 uses *ephistanai* (cp. I Thess 5.3 to be quoted presently), 21.35 *epeiserchesthai*. Both *ephistanai* and *eperchesthai* are favourite Lucan words; see Creed, The Gospel according to St. Luke, 1930, 258. On *eperchesthai* and *epeiserchesthai* in the New Testament see below, pp. 34ff.
[6] See below, p. 30, on Mk 13.36.
[7] Mt 24.50, Lk 12.46.

it may be recalled, is from early on associated with the sudden.[1]

According to I Thessalonians,[2] 'when they shall say, Peace and safety, then sudden destruction cometh upon them, as travail upon a woman with child'. Again, the reference is to the last judgment. 'Destruction' and 'to come upon'[3]—the old typical words connected with suddenness. Among the Old Testament texts in the background we should include those two from Jeremiah where people hope for peace 'and behold, be'atha, terror'; above we adverted to the possible etymological affinity between b't and petha'.[4]

In the preceding and following verses in I Thessalonians the day of the Lord is compared to 'a thief in the night'. The comparison recurs several times in the New Testament, but 'suddenness' is never introduced. This is hardly accidental. A thief may indeed break in when not expected, the element of 'not knowing the hour' is indeed there,[5] but a 'sudden' event is in addition striking, stunning, often violent. The onset of pangs of childbirth is 'sudden'. Admittedly, as time goes on, the simile of the thief gets more and more mixed up with others; so that in the later sources it would not be surprising to find 'suddenness' intruding.[6] In fact, however, the intrusion never takes place.

Aphno. On the first Christian Pentecost, 'suddenly there came from heaven a sound of a mighty wind', accompanying the descent of the Spirit.[7] When Paul and Silas were praying in jail at midnight, 'suddenly there was a great earthquake' opening the doors. [8] Finally, at Malta, a viper fastened on Paul's hand; he shook it off

---

[1] See above, p. 11.

[2] I Thess 5.3.

[3] *Ephistanai* as in Lk 21.34, above, p. 28.

[4] Jer 8.15, 14.19; see above, pp. 3, 19.

[5] Mt 24.43, Lk 12.39, Rev 3.3.

[6] Jesus, it seems, referred to an actual case, a man who had failed to protect his house from thieves; and the moral was that his listeners should be more far-sighted as to the judgment threatening them. Mt 24.43 and Lk 12.39 connect the judgment with the parousia. In I Thess 5.2, 4 the day of the Lord may overtake people like a thief—we are fast moving away from the concrete basis. In II Pet 3.10 the day of the Lord comes like a thief, and the heavens will pass away with great noise. Finally, in Rev 3.3, 16.15 Christ writes that he will come like a thief. See Jeremias, Die Gleichnisse Jesu, 6th ed., 1962, 45ff., and cp. below, p. 72.

[7] Acts 2.2.

[8] Acts 16.26. On the 'immediate' opening of the doors, see below, p. 44, under *parachrema*.

but the barbarians present expected him 'to fall down dead suddenly'[1].

At least in the first two passages there is no question of a disaster; this is not, or no longer, the necessary implication of *aphno*. What all three events, however, have in common is that they are of an awe-inspiring, supernatural character. They might all be called *exaisios*, 'terrible'—a word by which, as we saw, the LXX renders *pith'om*, 'suddenly', as well as *pl'*, 'wondrous', 'awesome'.[2] In the case of Paul and the viper, it is indeed a disaster that the barbarians feared. But even here it is more probably the 'wondrous' element to which *aphno* directs attention. They were enthused, we are told, when nothing *atopon*, 'strange', 'enormous', happened to Paul.[3] Of traditional associations with suddenness, we may note the nocturnal setting of the earthquake, and the words 'to fall' and 'dead' in the story of Paul and the viper. We shall come back below[4] to a certain aspect of this story.

Exaiphnes. 'Watch, lest coming suddenly he find you sleeping': Mark.[5] In a similar warning Luke, we just saw, has *aiphnidios*.[6] 'To come' is traditionally associated with the sudden,[7] and so is the setting which is at night.

In the Lucan birth narrative, 'and suddenly there was with the angel a multitude of the heavenly host'.[8] No disaster, to be sure, but neither a sweetly comfortable happening, no *gemütliche Weihnachtsabend in der warmen Stube*. A few verses previously[9] there is a first vision, of an angel surrounded by the glory of the Lord, which strikes terror into the shepherds. The angel calms them and announces the birth of the Saviour. Now, however, 'suddenly', a second vision, of the full heavenly army: surely, no less fearful than the first. (Even their proclamation 'Peace among men in whom he

---

[1] Acts 28.6.

[2] See above, pp. 14f.

[3] The New English Bible translates Acts 28.6: 'They still expected that any moment he would swell up or drop down dead'. This is inexact, first, in toning down 'suddenly' and thus losing the particular atmosphere evoked by the word, secondly, in making the adverb cover both the swelling and the dropping dead whereas, in the original, it qualifies only the latter.

[4] See p. 75.

[5] See Mk 13.36.

[6] Lk 21.34; see above, p. 28.

[7] Mark here uses *erchesthai*.

[8] Lk 2.13.

[9] Lk 2.9.

is well pleased' implies judgment as well as promise.[1]) The sense of *exaiphnes* is the same as that of *aphno*: the breaking in of the 'wondrous'. The setting is at night.[2]

The father of an epileptic describes his son's disease: 'A spirit taketh him and suddenly crieth out and teareth him that he foameth'.[3] Maybe it is the son who 'suddenly crieth out'—it makes little difference to the present argument. In the Marcan parallel the spirit shouts, not as it seizes the victim,[4] but as, at Jesus's command, it has to come out — and this shout is, of course, not sudden.[5] Luke's description of the seizure may be influenced by medical idiom.[6] At any rate, the adverb denotes a supernatural, demoniacal, sinister attack; the use is comparable to that of *aphno* in the story of Paul and the viper in Acts.[7] Matthew mentions no shout and, indeed, no spirit.[8]

The adverb occurs in two of the three accounts of Paul's conversion in Acts. The author writes: 'and suddenly there shone round him a light out of heaven and he fell upon the earth'.[9] Paul, in an address to the Jews of Jerusalem said to have been delivered in Hebrew,[10] declares: 'suddenly there shone from heaven a great light round about me, and I fell unto the ground'.[11] A supernatural, awe-inspiring event. Admittedly it involves judgment and even temporary blindness, but the point of *exaiphnes* is the unexpected impact of the 'wondrous'. Note the verb 'to fall', often connected with suddenness.

In the third account, where Paul speaks before Agrippa, *exaiphnes* is not found, nor the blindness.[12] It is hardly accidental that, whereas the two first accounts refer directly to what the super-

---

[1] See Lagrange, L'Evangile selon Saint Luc, 1921, 77.

[2] The New English Bible does less than justice to *exaiphnes* by translating 'All at once there was with the angel'. Rembrandt brings out splendidly the panic, at the angel's apparition, of shepherds, flocks, trees and earth. It is true that the heavenly host whom, somewhat anticipating, he shews circling the dove consists of attractive little angels.

[3] Lk 9.39.

[4] Mk 9.18, 20. On 'at once' in 9.20 see below, pp. 56f., under *euthys*.

[5] Mk 9.26.

[6] See Hobart, The Medical Language of St. Luke, 1882, 19.

[7] Acts 28.6; see above, p. 30.

[8] Mt 17.15ff.

[9] Acts 9.3f.

[10] Acts 21.40.

[11] Acts 22.6.

[12] Acts 26.13.

natural, the light, did—'there shone round about him (me) a light'—
the third concentrates on what Paul did—'I saw a light'.

Exapina. According to Mark, Elijah and Moses talk with the
transfigured Jesus, an apparition frightening the disciples. Then a
cloud overshadows the latter, and a voice declares: 'This is my
beloved son, hear him'. 'And suddenly', the text goes on, 'having
looked round about, they saw no man any more save Jesus only
with themselves'.[1] Here it is particularly important not to weaken
the force of the adverb. For in this version, it is the final sentence—
where the disciples see Jesus alone, Elijah and Moses having van-
ished—which constitutes the climax: it is an awesome revelation to
discover him as the one and only one designated by the voice, the
Old Testament prophets being 'no longer with them'. 'Suddenly'—a
striking, tremendous, 'wondrous' event. Mark is indeed somewhat
disquiet about the disciples' initial ignorance, reflected in Peter's
proposal of three tabernacles. He was so afraid, we are told, that
'he wist not what to say': this note is doubtless inserted as an excuse.[2]

In Matthew, it is no longer a revelation that the voice should
refer to Jesus and Jesus only. It is taken for granted that it could
refer to no one else. So the adverb 'suddenly' has no place in the
last sentence where the disciples see Jesus alone.[3] The point of the
narrative, from a singling out of Jesus, shifts to something in the
nature of an epiphany. Moses and Elijah talk with the transfigured
Jesus: no mention of fright at this stage. Peter, in proposing three
tabernacles, addresses Jesus as 'Lord', not, as in Mark, as 'Rabbi'.[4]
There come the cloud and the voice, and it is on hearing the voice
that the disciples are frightened and indeed fall on their faces,
clearly in worship.[5] From this culmination the line descends. Jesus
bids them arise and calms them: no such calming before the final
sentence in Mark, far from it. Then: 'and having lifted up their
eyes they saw no man save Jesus only'.[6] The particle 'any longer'
is dropped: the point here is not the revelation that as the Old
Testament prophets are 'no longer with them' Jesus alone must
be meant by the voice, this ending in Matthew means restoration of

---

[1] Mk 9.8.
[2] Mk 9.6.
[3] Mt 17.8.
[4] Mt 17.4, Mk 9.5.
[5] For possible influences from Dan 8.17f., 10.7ff., and an echo in Rev
1.17, see Lagrange, L'Evangile selon Saint Marc, 2nd ed., 1947, 232.
[6] Mt 17.8.

the normal relationship after the epiphany. It is quite different from Mark.

Lohmeyer remarks on the Marcan ending: *So ist jetzt auch den Worten nach die alte Verbundenheit wieder hergestellt.*[1] This is absolutely correct—for the Matthean ending. But where it stands, it constitutes an assimilation of Mark to Matthew. The tendency, as may be expected, started early. D has *euthys*, 'at once', 'in due course', instead of *exapina*, 'suddenly', in Mark.[2] This is not merely substitution of a commoner word; it is also a toning down.

Luke agrees with Mark in a vital respect: it is emphasized—not taken for granted—that the voice designates Jesus and no one besides. Only this is conveyed, not in the form of a 'wondrous' revelation to the disciples, but in a factual, impersonal style: 'And as the voice occurred—or, had occurred—Jesus was found—or, found himself—alone'. No room here for 'suddenly'.[3] The problems raised by Luke's choice of this mode of report—as well as by other peculiarities of his version—lie beyond the scope of this study.

The extent to which Mark stands out can be demonstrated from a different angle. Except for his account of the transfiguration, 'suddenly' is never used in the Bible — Old Testament or New — of the disappearance, the ending, of a supernatural display. It is the unlooked for opening which startles, which is 'sudden'. 'And suddenly there was with the angel a multitude of the heavenly host.'[4] A supernatural display indeed ends as abruptly as it begins: it is all the more significant that where this is brought out, it is done otherwise than by 'suddenly'. The vessel shewn to Peter in Acts 'was at once received up into heaven', *euthys*, the angel delivering him from prison 'at once departed from him', *eutheos*.[5] The Marcan transfiguration is unique—because, for once, it is a disappearance which is the really shocking thing, the disappearance of Moses and Elijah; of course, it coincides with the positive 'seeing Jesus only with themselves' as the beloved Son to be heard.

In the whole of the New Testament, then, 'sudden' or 'suddenly' is met in two areas only. One is eschatology—the last judgment

---

[1] Das Evangelium des Markus, 1937, 177.

[2] See below, p. 56, under *euthys*.

[3] Lk 9.36. The translation of the New English Bible, 'was seen to be alone', is a fierce assimilation to Matthew and Mark.

[4] Lk 2.13. Or 'The Lord spoke suddenly unto Moses and Aaron and Miriam', Nu 12.4. See above, pp. 30f., 3, and below, p, 72.

[5] Acts 10.16, 12.10; see below, p. 70.

may overtake man in this way. Three passages belong here, one from Mark,[1] one from Luke,[2] and one from I Thessalonians.[3] We have also quoted a saying from Matthew and Luke which, though not containing the word, gives as precise a definition as one might ask for;[4] and further approximations, both from the Synoptics and the Epistles, might be added. The other area is that of supernatural, awesome occurrences, with eight passages: one from Mark,[5] two from Luke,[6] and five from Acts.[7]

In the area of eschatology, we conclude, there is a common strand in the Synoptics—with an old Jewish tradition behind it—where the sudden arrival of the supreme moment is stressed. It is a strand which, both in the gospels and in the Jewish sources, is capable of being isolated (more or less), expressing a (more or less) definite attitude and its development. The absence of the notion from John is significant, as is that of, say, the related notion 'to watch'. (Neither *agrypnein* nor *gregorein* is found.) John's historical and theological starting-point leads him away from this kind of suddenness.

The use of the terms with reference to 'wondrous' events is so rare that little can be said by way of comparison between various writers. Luke is conceivably a little more inclined to this use than the other evangelists (owing to his medical background?). That Mark alone has it in the transfiguration means nothing since there are special reasons for its omission by Matthew and Luke—and John omits the entire pericope.

2. 'To come upon'

It may be useful to consider the fate in the New Testament of the more interesting remaining Septuagintal words for 'sudden' or 'suddenly' though, in the New Testament, they have not this meaning: *eperchesthai* or *epeiserchesthai*, *parachrema* and *euthys*, *eutheos*. *Eisapax* and *exaisios* do not occur in the New Testament;[8]

---

[1] Mk 13.36.

[2] Lk 21.34.

[3] I Thess 5.3.

[4] Mt 24.50, Lk 12.46.

[5] Mk 9.8, transfiguration.

[6] Lk 2.13, heavenly host, 9.39, epileptic.

[7] Acts 2.2, Pentecost, 9.3, Paul, 16.26, earthquake, 22.6, Paul, 28.6, viper.

[8] *Atopos*, however, in the story of Paul and the viper, Acts 28.6, above, p. 30, is not far from *exaisios*.

they are infrequent enough in the Old. On *spoude* and *tachys* we
have nothing fresh to say; except, with regard to the former, that
the New Testament contains no vestige of the unpleasant sense
discernible in the LXX and, here and there, in the Apocrypha
harking back to it.[1] Luke's *stigme chronou* we shall briefly comment
on in the last but one section of this study.[2]

The first of the terms to be discussed, 'to come upon', is a Lucan
favourite. It is used either in connection with disasters or threats
of disasters or in connection with awe-inspiring occurrences. We
come across one exception, in Ephesians, in the technical phrase
'the coming ages'.[3] Even this phrase has its ultimate origin in an
eschatological setting.

The verb is found ten times: four times in Luke (including the
only passage with *epeiserchesthai*[4]), four times in Acts, once in
Ephesians—in the text just cited—and once in James.

In two passages we have to do with a 'wondrous' event, in fact,
the same event in both—the descent of the Spirit. There is the annunciation, 'The Holy Ghost will come upon thee',[5] and there is
the promise to the disciples prior to Pentecost, 'But ye shall receive
power when the Holy Ghost is come upon you'.[6] It may be recalled
that, on Pentecost, 'suddenly there came from heaven a sound'.[7]

In two passages it is a question of an attack: in Luke's simile
of Jesus's superiority over Satan, 'But when a stronger shall come
upon him, he taketh from him his armour',[8] and in a scene in Acts
where 'the Jews came' to stone Paul.[9] The Matthean and Marcan
parallel to Luke's simile is slightly different and the verb does not
occur.[10]

We may here insert a remark on *phthanein epi* employed in this
pericope by Matthew and Luke. (The sentence is not in Mark, so
it is Q whatever that may mean.) 'If I cast out devils, then the
kingdom of God is come upon you'.[11] In the Greek Old Testament,

---

[1] See above, pp. 18ff.
[2] Below, pp. 75f.
[3] Eph 2.7; cp. Hermas, Vision 4.3.5.
[4] Lk 21.35.
[5] Lk 1.35.
[6] Acts 1.8.
[7] Acts 2.2; see above, pp. 29f.
[8] Lk 11.22.
[9] Acts 14.19.
[10] Mt 12.29, Mk 3.27.
[11] Mt 12.28, Lk 11.20.

the expression invariably has an adverse sense[1]; and so it has in the only other New Testament text where it occurs, I Thessalonians,[2] 'For the wrath is come upon them (the Jews) to the uttermost'. It is highly probable that the kingdom in the Beelzebub controversy means in the first place condemnation, defeat, ruin, of the opponents addressed: 'has overtaken you' rather than the usual English 'is come unto you',[3] the German *ist zu euch gekommen*, the French *vous est arrivé*. The contact between the controversy and I Thessalonians is more than purely verbal.

There remain five passages in all of which *eperchesthai* is used of calamity. One is the request of Simon Magus, cursed by Peter: 'Pray for me that none of these things come upon me'.[4]

The other four are concerned with eschatology. Luke speaks of 'men's hearts failing them for fear and for looking after those things which are coming upon the earth'.[5] Note the 'fear'—often met, we saw, in this context. The sentence is not paralleled in Matthew or Mark,[6] but it may well be taken from traditional material: 'the things which are coming upon the earth' is a Rabbinic phrase.[7]

In the concluding part of this chapter, Luke has the warning with *aiphnidios* discussed above: 'lest that day come upon you as a sudden one, as a snare'. 'To come upon' here *ephistanai*. He goes on: 'For it shall come upon all them that dwell on the face of the earth', *epeiserchesthai*.[8] This illustrates well the force of the verb—or at least of the strengthened form *epeiserchesthai*—which, without any further qualification, will convey the threatening, desperate aspect of the happening. 'It shall come upon' is quite enough to evoke

---

[1] Jud 20.34, 'they knew not that evil was coming upon them'; 20.42, 'and the battle came upon them'; Ec 8.14, 'upon the just there cometh according to the work of the wicked'—significantly, in the second half of the verse, alluding to undeserved prosperity, the preposition is not *epi* but *pros*; Dan (Theodotion) 4.21, 'this is the decree of the most High which is come upon my lord the king'; 4.28, 'all this came upon the king Nebuchadnezzar'.

[2] I Thess 2.16.

[3] The New English Bible correctly puts 'upon'. The thesis here propounded, incidentally, is neither for nor against Aalen's interpretation of *basileia* in New Testament Studies 8, 1962, 215ff.; the present text is discussed on p. 230.

[4] Acts 8.24.

[5] Lk 21.26.

[6] Mt 24.29ff., Mk 13.24ff.

[7] See Strack-Billerbeck, Kommentar zum Neuen Testament aus Talmud und Midrasch, vol. 2, 1924, 255, 358, vol. 4, pt. 2, 1928, 985 etc.

[8] Lk 22.34f.; see above, p. 28.

this sinister element. It is interesting that, instead of 'lest that day
come upon you suddenly as a snare, for it shall come upon all',
some MSS read 'lest that day come upon you suddenly, for as a
snare it shall come upon all'. This is manifestly an 'easier reading'.
The particular force of *epeiserchesthai* is not, or no longer, sufficient.
So, in order to make the day not only universal but also menacing,
the words 'as a snare' are attached to this verb.

According to Acts, Paul preached to the Jews of Antioch: 'Beware
lest that come upon you which is spoken of in the prophets—Behold
ye despisers and wonder and perish, for I work a work in your days
which ye shall in no wise believe though a man declare it unto
you'.[1] The quotation 'Behold' etc. is from Habakkuk.[2] In the
Dead Sea Commentary on Habakkuk the expression 'to come upon'
occurs twice in the discussion of this verse: 'all that is coming upon
the last generation', 'all that is coming upon God's people'.[3] More than
that, the verse is interpreted as directed against those not believing
in the words of the Teacher of Righteousness, the New Covenant,
the things 'coming upon' the world in its final phase.

A third bond between Acts and the Dead Sea Scrolls is worth a
mention. The Massoretic Hebrew text of Habakkuk reads 'Behold
among the nations', *baggoyim*, whereas Acts, 'Behold ye despisers',
follows the LXX, *hoi kataphronetai*; in Hebrew this would presup-
pose *habboghedhim* or *boghedhim*, not very remote from the Massoretic. (It should be remembered that vowels are not written.)
Now it is clear that the Dead Sea Commentator, if he had not
'despisers' before him, at least interpreted what lay before him in
just this sense. Three times we find the actual word (*hab*)*boghedhim*:
the quotation from Habakkuk, we are informed, envisages 'the
despisers with the Man of the Lie', 'the despisers of the New Covenant', 'the despisers at the end of days'.[4] Translators prefer
'traitors' or 'unfaithful'. The argument here advanced is not affected

---

[1] Acts 13.40f.
[2] Hab 1.5; cp. Is 29.14.
[3] 2.7, 10, in the Scroll, with *ba' 'al* for 'to come upon': *kol habba'oth 'al*,
'all that is coming upon'. The expression recurs in 7.1, where Hab 2.1f.
is discussed: 'and God told Habakkuk to write down that which was coming
upon the last generation'. No reference to the Dead Sea Scrolls is given in
the fairly recent commentary on Acts by Haenchen, Die Apostelgeschichte,
13th ed., 1961, 355.
[4] 2.1, 3, 5, in the Scroll.

if we adopt this rendering—only it should then also be adopted for Paul's speech in Acts.

There can be no doubt that Paul gives Habakkuk an application —or is represented as giving it an application—the main outline of which was already established; the main outline and, indeed, some detail of importance as well, including the concept of 'to come upon'.

Lastly, James—'Ye rich, weep and howl for your spoilings that are coming upon you'.[1] Note 'spoiling', at home, we observed, in the province of suddenness.

It will be noted that *eperchesthai* does not figure in Matthew, Mark or John. However, the passages where it does figure offer too small a basis for comparison. So nothing will be said here as to any possible significance of the concentration in Luke and Acts.

3. 'STRAIGHTWAY'

a) General

Parachrema occurs eighteen times in the New Testament: twice in Matthew—though, as both times it refers to the same event in the same pericope,[2] for the purpose of establishing relative frequency we might count this as one emphatic application—apart from this only in Luke—ten times—and Acts—six. Luke evidently has a predilection for it. The word is common in medical treatises.[3] But though this may be an initial cause, it does not fully account for the way Luke uses it, which is far more specialised. In the medical treatises, for example, we find not only that a disease will 'straight-way' have such and such consequences but also that certain reme-dies should be applied 'straightway'.[4] The latter usage is not paralleled in Luke. It is likely that, whatever first determined his choice, his handling of the adverb largely reflects his own theolo-gical or stylistic bias.

In the New Testament the word does not mean 'suddenly'; it means 'straightway', 'forthwith'. None the less there are some note-worthy connotations linking it loosely to that sphere. Above all, the element of the 'wondrous' is present in all eighteen passages.

---

[1] Ja 5.1. The New English Bible 'descending on you': why?.
[2] Mt 21.19f.
[3] Hobart, op. cit., 96ff.
[4] Hippocrates, Opera Omnia, per Anutium Foesium, 1624, Intern. Af-fect., 551, line 7—among Hobart's quotations.

On closer analysis it may be affirmed that, in seventeen out of the eighteen—the exception being the death of Agrippa in Acts[1]—it is a question of immediate miraculous actualisation of an order or prediction of Jesus, or one in Jesus's name, or some influence emanating from Jesus, or the impact of the Spirit.[2]

b) Matthew

In the Matthean cursing of the fig-tree, as distinct from the Marcan (no parallel in Luke or John), it is stressed that no interval elapsed between the curse and its effect. Jesus condemned the tree, 'and straightway it withered away'; and this feature is mentioned again in the reaction of the disciples, who 'marvelled, saying, How is it straightway withered away?'.[3] In Mark, Jesus curses the tree, then intervenes the cleansing of the Temple, and it is on the following day that he and the disciples pass by again and the latter notice that the tree is destroyed.

The double *parachrema* in Matthew is directed against such a version, whether the Marcan itself or one similar in this respect. The response, for Matthew, was immediate and he is concerned to leave no doubt about it. The rendering 'suddenly' would obviously miss the point: the difference between it and *parachrema* is here well illumined.

The problem is how Matthew in this one pericope comes to use a term otherwise confined to Luke and Acts, where indeed it is frequent in precisely this sense. If elsewhere the term occurred in Luke only, one might argue that it is favoured by Q and that the episode of the fig-tree is Q though not appearing in Luke. But this line is closed owing to the frequency of the term in Acts. So why does Matthew not use *euthys*, as in more than fifteen other cases? The explanation may be that, in the episode of the fig-tree, where he attaches such importance to the immediacy of the response, he chooses *parachrema* because *euthys*, as we shall see, is not quite so unambiguous: we shall see that, though basically signifying 'at once', sometimes it means little more than 'in due course'. It is true that this latter meaning is Marcan rather than Matthean, still *parachrema* is stronger.[4]

---

[1] Acts 12.23; see below, pp. 45f.
[2] Cp. Lagrange, L'Evangile selon Saint Luc, 1921, 152.
[3] Mt 21.19f., Mk 11.11ff.
[4] On *euthys*, see below, pp. 46ff.

c) Luke

According to Luke, the angel Gabriel told Zacharias that he would be dumb 'until the day that these things shall have come to pass';[1] and in fact, when the son was born and named John, 'his mouth was opened straightway'.[2] It might perhaps be objected that the angel announced not that, as soon as the things had come about, Zacharias would be able to speak, but that till then he would be unable. But this would be to impose too pedantic an interpretation on the narrative. We shall meet a very similar fulfilment of a prediction, 'straightway' at the end of a term, in Luke's version of the cock-crow.[3]

On Jesus's rebuking the fever that had befallen Simon's mother-in-law, 'it left her and straightway she got up and ministered unto them'.[4] One might just conceivably translate 'and straightway, having got up, she ministered'. But a comparison with other Lucan pericopes renders this interpretation unlikely.[5] The parallel in Matthew has no such adverb,[6] that in Mark perhaps has *eutheos*, 'at once', with 'it left her'.[7] We shall see that Luke substitutes *parachrema* in several places.[8]

The man sick with palsy, at Jesus's command, 'having straightway risen up before them, having taken up that whereon he lay, departed to his house'.[9] Again, conceivably, we might translate 'straightway, having risen, he departed', but it is implausible. No such adverb in Matthew,[10] *euthys* in Mark:[11] one of the cases where Luke substitutes *parachrema*.[12]

In the story of the woman with an issue of blood *parachrema* occurs twice. She touched Jesus's garment 'and straightway her issue stanched'. Jesus noticed that some power had emanated from

---

[1] Lk 1.20.
[2] Lk 1.64.
[3] Lk 22.60; see below, pp. 42f.
[4] Lk 4.39.
[5] E.g. Lk 8.55, where 'straightway' must refer to the getting up, no other verb being there.
[6] Mt 8.15.
[7] Mk 1.31; see below, pp. 49f.
[8] Lk 5.25, 8.44, 8.55, 18.43, 22.60; see this and the following pages.
[9] Lk 5.25.
[10] Mt 9.7.
[11] Mk 2.12; see below, pp. 50f.
[12] See Lk 4.39 just discussed.

him, upon which the woman proclaimed that she had touched him 'and was healed straightway'.[1] Jesus dismissed her in peace: 'Thy faith hath made thee whole'.

In Matthew, the woman touches Jesus, he assures her 'Thy faith hath made thee whole', and now follows the statement: 'And she was made whole from that hour'.[2] This or similar phrases are employed in the same sense in other Matthean narratives;[3] and John elaborates the meaning in connection with the healing of the centurion's servant.[4] We shall come across a passage in Acts[5] where 'in that hour' and *parachrema* are synonymous.

In Mark, the woman touches Jesus and 'at once, *euthys*, her blood was dried up'.[6] So Luke's *parachrema* replaces *euthys*.[7] When we come to her confession in Mark, this adverb is not repeated, we are simply informed that 'she told him all the truth'. There is less emphasis on the point, it seems, than in Luke. There is indeed a second *euthys* in the Marcan version: Jesus 'at once' noticed that power had emanated from him. We shall discuss this below.[8]

Jairus's daughter was told to arise; 'and her spirit came again and she arose straightway'.[9] Matthew has no such adverb,[10] and Mark has *euthys* (followed in the same verse by another *euthys*, 'and they were at once astonished').[11] Another Lucan substitution of *parachrema*.[12]

The woman with a spirit of infirmity, when Jesus laid hands on her, 'was straightway made straight'.[13] No parallels in the other gospels.

Bartimaeus was told 'Look up, thy faith hath made thee whole'. 'And straightway he looked up'.[14] In the Matthean parallel we find

---

[1] Lk 8.44, 47.
[2] Mt 9.22.
[3] Mt 8.13, 15.28, 17.18.
[4] Jn 4.52f. The response in 19.27 deserves attention.
[5] Acts 16.33; cp. 16.18, 22.13. See below, pp. 44f. On Acts 22.13 we shall comment at the end of this division of *parachrema*; see below, p. 45.
[6] Mk 5.29; see below, p. 53.
[7] Cp. Lk 4.39, above, p. 40.
[8] See p. 53.
[9] Lk 8.55.
[10] Mt 9.25.
[11] Mk 5.42; see below, pp. 53f.
[12] See above, p. 40, in connection with Lk 4.39.
[13] Lk 13.13.
[14] Lk 18.43.

eutheos, in the Marcan *euthys,* 'at once'[1]. Luke has substituted his *parachrema.*

Surely, in the Lucan introduction of the parable of the pounds *parachrema* expresses the same idea as in the texts discussed so far. Jesus seeks and obtains hospitality from Zacchaeus, a publican, which sets people complaining. Yet Jesus says to Zacchaeus: 'This day is salvation come to this house, forsomuch as he also is a son of Abraham'. That this is intended to be a public proclamation as well as a communication to Zacchaeus is clear from the third person: 'he is a son of Abraham'.[2] Jesus goes on: 'For the Son of Man is come to seek and save that which was lost'. Then he offers a parable 'because he was nigh to Jerusalem and because they thought that the kingdom of God should appear straightway'.[3] They (whoever they may have been) thought so, that is, in reliance on the power of Jesus's word—'This day' etc. No parallels in the other gospels.

Lagrange translates *sur-le-champ,* interpreting it as *soudainement;* and he does not list this text among the illustrations of the typically Lucan use of *parachrema.*[4] But this is to tear the verse from what precedes it in the evangelist: after Jesus's proclamation, a fulfilment 'straightway' was expected. Not a 'sudden' one; 'straightway' in the Lucan sense of immediate response. The New English Bible errs in the opposite direction, translating 'at any moment'. This is too non-committal.

In Luke, Jesus's prediction to Peter is: 'The cock shall not crow this day before that thou shalt thrice deny that thou knowest me'.[5] As Peter is making his third denial, 'straightway, while he yet spake, the cock crew'.[6] Matthew and Mark formulate the prediction a little differently: 'This night, before the cock crow (twice, in Mark), thou shalt deny me thrice'.[7] (As far as the point here relevant is concerned, John agrees with Luke.[8]) In both Matthew and Mark (as also in John), 'at once', *euthys* (*eutheos* in John), 'the cock crew' ('the second time', in Mark).[9]

---

[1] Mt 20.34, Mk 10.52; see below, pp. 57, 60, footnote 6.
[2] See Creed, op. cit., 231.   [3] Lk 19.11.
[4] L'Evangile selon Saint Luc, 1921, 152, 492f.
[5] Lk 22.34.   [6] Lk 22.60.   [7] Mt 26.34, Mk 14.30.
[8] Jn 13.38; there are divergences, but the decisive 'shall not before' recurs.
[9] Mt 26.74, Mk 14.72, Jn 18.27. In some MSS a first cock-crow, without 'at once', in Mk 14.68.

Parachrema, substituted by Luke for *euthys*[1], has its full, characteristic force. We pointed out above that the pattern is the same as in the story of Zacharias, who was to be dumb till certain things had come about and then 'straightway' spoke.[2] This pattern accounts for Luke's formulation of the prediction in the present case: the cock was restrained till the appropriate moment and then 'straightway' crew. Whether the formulation of the prediction is Luke's work or whether he chose it from several alternatives already current we shall not attempt to decide, especially as the Johannine problem would be involved.

This exact fulfilment of the prediction is further underlined in Luke by two additions. First, the cock crew 'while he yet spake'. Secondly, 'the Lord turned and looked upon Peter'.[3] It is true that from here onwards Luke falls in, in the main, with the other Synoptics—Peter remembers essentially the Matthean and Marcan formulation, 'Before the cock crow, thou shalt deny me thrice'.[4] This may be simply lack of consistency on Luke's part; but it is not impossible that we have to do with post-Lucan assimilation.[5]

d) Acts

In Acts, Peter, in the name of Jesus, commands a lame man to walk and lifts him up: 'and straightway his feet received strength'.[6]

Sapphira is told by Peter that she is doomed to instant death, having tempted the Spirit of the Lord: 'and she fell down straightway'.[7]

Paul, 'filled with the Holy Ghost', tells the sorcerer Elymas that 'the hand of the Lord is upon you and thou shalt be blind, and straightway there fell on him a mist'.[8] D substitutes the commoner *eutheos*, 'at once.[9]

On the other hand, D inserts the double phrase *parachrema eutheos* into a healing at Lystra. Paul told a cripple to stand upright,

---

[1] See above, p. 40, in connection with Lk 4.39.
[2] Lk 1.64; see above, p. 40.
[3] Lk 22.61.
[4] Lk 22.61.
[5] Lk 22.62 is widely regared as assimilated to Mt 26.75; see Rengstorf, Das Evangelium nach Lukas, 9th ed., 1962, 259.
[6] Acts 3.7.
[7] Acts 5.10.
[8] Acts 13.11.
[9] See below, under *euthys*, p. 70.

'and he leaped and walked', D: 'and straightway at once he leaped
and walked'.[1] This pleonasm is classical,[2] but D has clearly imported
the adverbs from similar stories. We have not included this text
in our statistics of *parachrema* presented above.[3]

In the story of Paul and Silas in prison at Philippi, *parachrema*
occurs twice. At midnight, suddenly (*aphno*) there was an earthquake shaking the foundations, 'and straightway all the doors were
opened and everyone's bands were loosed'.[4] The 'sudden' earthquake
implies action by God or the Spirit. We found a 'sudden' sound as
of a mighty wind portending the descent of the Spirit on Pentecost,[5]
and on another occasion its descent is marked by an earthquake—
in fact, an earthquake following the prayer of Peter, John and their
company,[6] just as that at Philippi follows the prayer of Peter and
Silas. It emerges that *parachrema* here, too, denotes the immediate
result of divine intervention. The latter itself is 'sudden', and then,
'straightway', comes its effect: the difference between the two
concepts is here once again neatly illustrated.

The jailer and his family readily listen to Paul's and Silas's
preaching; 'and he took them the same hour of the night and washed
their stripes, and was baptized, he and all his, straightway'.[7] Considering the numerous passages we have inspected, it is very plausible that the quick conversion, 'the same hour of the night',
'straightway', is being represented as taking place under the direct
impact of the Spirit, the power revealed in the earthquake and
also, maybe, in the staying behind of all prisoners so that the jailer's
life is saved. We must not forget that in quite a few cases where
a person is 'straightway' healed through Jesus's word or influence,
belief and acknowledgment are virtually part of the cure.[8] In the
case of Simon's mother-in-law, if we punctuated—improbably—
'and straightway, having got up, she ministered unto them', the
adverb would be directly connected with entry into the service of
Jesus.[9] The ministering is indeed not quite unparalleled in the nar-

---

[1] Acts 14.10; see below, under *euthys*, p. 70.
[2] Blass-Debrunner, Neutestamentliche Grammatik, 5th ed., 1921, 282.
[3] See p. 38.
[4] Acts 16.26.; see above, pp. 29f., for a discussion of *aphno* in this text.
[5] Acts 2.2, see above, p. 29.
[6] Acts 4.31.
[7] Acts 16.33.
[8] Lk 4.39, 5.25, 8.47, 13.13, 18.43, Acts 3.7f.; see above, pp. 40f., 43.
[9] Lk 4.39; see above, p. 40.

rative under review: the jailer takes Paul and Silas into his house, washes their stripes, is baptized, gives them food and believes.

'In that hour' and 'straightway' are practically synonymous in this narrative. The former phrase is used in this sense in two other passages in Acts.[1] One, concerning Paul's cure from blindness, we shall consider presently.

This cure is mentioned twice. The first time we are told how Ananias, sent by Jesus, lays hands on Paul: 'And at once (*eutheos*) there fell from his eyes as it were scales and he looked up'.[2] There is a variant reading: 'and straightway, *parachrema*, he looked up'. Its support, however, is very slight. We may take it that in one line of transmission of the gospel *parachrema* has been added by way of assimilation to narratives like that of Bartimaeus.[3] In the statistics of *parachrema* set out above this text is not included,[4] though it would, of course, make a perfect fourteenth to the thirteen in this division.

Let us note, however, that whoever added *parachrema* probably felt justified by the subsequent second account of the cure: 'in that very hour I looked up on him'.[5] 'In that hour', as just pointed out, is very close to 'straightway'.

e) *Luke and Acts*

This leaves one passage only in Acts where *parachrema* has not the peculiar meaning found in all the seventeen others; namely, the account of Herod Agrippa's death. He delivered a public oration, and the people declared his voice to be that of a god: 'and straightway the angel of the Lord smote him, because he gave not God the glory, and he was eaten of worms and gave up the ghost'.[6] Here we are not told that what happened 'straightway' happened in response to a divine command or prediction. Indeed the word appears to signify something not remote from 'suddenly'.

Perhaps the solution lies in the fact that, whereas all the other seventeen texts are concerned with Jesus and his followers, that

---

[1] Acts 16.18, 22.13. For the gospels, see above, p. 41, in connection with Lk 8.44, 47.

[2] Acts 9.18; see below, p. 69.

[3] Lk 18.43; see above, pp. 41f.

[4] See above, p. 38.

[5] Acts 22.13; see above, p. 41, footnote 5.

[6] Acts 12.23.

before us concerns an outsider. It may be taken over from some source without much adaptation of the vocabulary to the rest of Acts.

There is, however, just a possibility that appearances are deceptive and that the sense here is less exceptional than one might believe at first sight. In Josephus[1] the king, having accepted praise belonging only to God, first sees the bird whose coming, he knows, announces his death within five days,[2] then his fatal illness seizes him. If Acts draws on some such version, the *parachrema* might be put under its influence even though—for very understandable reasons—the prediction was suppressed.

It can hardly be denied that *parachrema*, with its pregnant sense, has a definite place in Lucan theology, is part of a message he wishes to convey. Let us add that the reaction of observers to the result occurring 'straightway' is marvel, *thaumazo*,[3] fear, *phobos*,[4] ecstasy, *ekstasis, existemi*,[5] astonishnemt, *ekplessomai*.[6]

4. 'AT ONCE'

a) *Mark*

Euthys or *eutheos* is found between forty and fifty times in Mark, between fifteen and twenty in Matthew, seven times in Luke, six in John, some ten in Acts, and once in each Galatians, James, III John and Revelation. The word never means 'suddenly'. Indeed we shall see that at least in Mark and texts drawing on him, it often means less —or, according as one looks at it, more—than 'at once'. We begin with Mark.

Jesus was baptized; 'and at once, coming up out of the water, he saw the heavens rent and the Spirit descending'.[7] The adverb here denotes the immediacy of the event: we may recall that in Jewish proselyte baptism, 'he immerses and comes up—behold, he is like an Israelite in all respects'.[8]

---

[1] Ant. 19.8.2.346.
[2] Ant. 18.6.7.200.
[3] Mt 21.20; see above, p. 39.
[4] Lk 1.65, Acts 5.11; see above, pp. 40, 43.
[5] Lk 5.26, 8.56; see above, pp. 40f.
[6] Acts 13.12; see above, p. 43.
[7] Mk 1.10.
[8] Bab. Yebamoth 47b. The New English Bible translates well: 'At the moment when he came up, he saw'.

D omits *euthys*. Maybe the scribe mistakenly connected it with 'coming up': 'and at once coming up, he saw'. That seemed queer—why ever should he not come up at once?—so it was simplest to drop the adverb. At any rate Matthew must have divided Mark in this erroneous way, hence: 'baptized, Jesus at once came up'.[1] (To be sure, Matthew goes on: 'and behold (*idou*) the heavens were rent'.) The scheme of the Marcan passage, with a participle between 'at once' and the verb it qualifies, recurs in over fifteen other texts in Mark, plus, maybe, three times in Matthew independently of Mark; never in Luke, John or Acts.[2]

Luke, besides other changes, omits *euthys* and also the technical reference to the 'coming up'.[3] John is not really comparable.[4] Let us note in passing first, that all attempts to dissociate New Testament baptism from Jewish proselyte baptism—futile on numerous grounds—break to pieces against this technical term, 'to come up', *'ala*, having its full force in Mark, a little weaker in Matthew, suppressed by Luke; and secondly, that the Matthean version, making Jesus 'come up at once,' affords conclusive proof of some use at least by Matthew of a written Mark — it cannot be accounted for in any other way.

The baptism ended in divine acknowledgment: 'and at once the spirit driveth him into the wilderness'.[5] Here *euthys* cannot be pressed; Matthew does not lose much by substituting 'then', *tote*,[6] though there is in *kai euthys* a trace of 'in due course', 'as had to happen after what preceded', 'and so'. It is less purely temporary, more theological, than *tote*; it is reminiscent of *oun* in one of its applications. The German *alsbald* is not a bad rendering, the New English Bible translates well 'Thereupon the Spirit sent him away'. Luke puts the noncommittal connecting particle *de*.[7] No parallel in John.

Jesus bade Simon and Andrew follow him, 'and at once, leaving

---

[1] Mt 3.16; see below, pp. 60, footnote 6, 61.

[2] Here are the other cases: Mk 1.18 (where Mt 4.20 again mispunctuates); 1.21; 1.29; 2.8; 2.12; 5.30; 5.36; 6.27; 6.54; 7.25; 8.10; 9.8 in D; 9.15; 9.24; 11.2; 14.43 (more or less); 14.45; 15.1. The three Matthean texts are: Mt 14.31; 25.15f.; 27.48. See this and the following pages.

[3] Lk 3.21.

[4] Jn 1.32ff.

[5] Mk 1.12.

[6] Mt 4.1.

[7] Lk 4.1.

their nets, they followed him'[1]. Doubtless a tribute to their readiness, but also, more generally, an indication of how things follow one another as they must, 'and duly'.

Matthew again seems to divide wrongly, 'and these, at once leaving their nets, followed him'.[2] It is not certain, but a comma after *hoi de* is more natural than after *hoi de eutheos*.[3] The New English Bible takes it in this sense: 'They left their nets at once and followed him'. Alas, it also assimilates Mark: 'And at once they left their nets and followed him'. Fortunately in this episode, as opposed to that of the baptism, the sense is not fundamentally affected. In Luke and John the call is told quite differently and *euthys* does not occur.[4]

The role of *euthys* as simply (or not so simply, according as one looks at it) indicating the *planmässige*, steady, blow upon blow succession of events comes out clearly in the next few verses. Soon after gaining Simon and Andrew Jesus saw the sons of Zebedee: 'and at once he called them, and, leaving their father, they went after him'.[5] Here the call, not the response to it, occurs 'at once'. The narrative goes on: 'And they go into Capernaum and at once on the sabbath day, entering into the synagogue, he taught'.[6] Even more schematically: 'And at once there was in the synagogue a man with an unclean spirit'.[7]

Matthew, in the call of the sons of Zebedee, gives 'at once' a—for him—more meaningful position, namely, the position it has in the call of Simon and Andrew: 'and he called them and these, at once leaving, followed him'.[8] No parallel in Luke or John. The notices about teaching at Capernaum and the man with an unclean spirit are not paralleled in Matthew or John, and Luke omits 'at once' both times.[9]

The New English Bible cuts out 'at once' from both the two first Marcan texts: 'he called them', 'and on the Sabbath he went to the synagogue and began to teach'.[10]This is not only to lose the

---

[1] Mk 1.18.

[2] Mt 4.20; see below, pp. 60, footnote 6, 61.

[3] Cp. Mt 4.22, to be discussed presently, on the same page.

[4] Lk 5.1ff., Jn 1.40ff.

[5] Mk 1.20.

[6] Mk 1.21.

[7] Mk 1.23.

[8] Mt 4.22; *hoi de eutheos* as in 4.20, just discussed. See also below, p. 60, footnote 6.

[9] Lk 4.31, 33.   [10] Mk 1.20, 21.

flavour of Mark's style—at least partly based on his theology—but also to obscure the relation between the various gospels. It makes it look as if Matthew, where he says that 'they left at once', freely added the 'at once'.[1] In the third Marcan text the New English Bible actually replaces 'and at once' by 'now'—'Now there was a man'[2]— thus creating the impression of a break where Mark emphasizes continuity; and, of course, it makes Mark look as smooth as Luke.[3]

As a result of Capernaum, Jesus's fame 'went out at once'.[4] A bit conventional, but it does stress the immediacy of the effect. Luke omits it.[5] No parallel in Matthew or John.

In the following verse we are told: 'And at once, having gone out of the synagogue, they went into the house of Simon and Andrew'.[6] 'At once' is not to be pressed; the meaning approaches 'in due course'. D omits it. So do Matthew and Luke.[7] No parallel in John.

Simon's mother-in-law was ill, 'and at once they tell him about her'.[8] Even here, the meaning is perhaps rather 'and so', 'and as had duly to happen'. The notice is not represented in Matthew;[9] it is in Luke but he omits the adverb.[10] No parallel in John.

In the following verse, Jesus raised her up 'and the fever left her at once'.[11] The adverb here denotes the immediacy of the cure. To be sure, it is missing from important MSS,[12] as also from Matthew.[13] But Luke may well have read it: 'And it left her, and straightway (*parachrema*) she arose'.[14] The substitution of *parachrema* for *euthys*, we saw, is frequent in Luke; and his transfer of the adverb from

---

[1] Mt 4.22.
[2] Mk 1.23.
[3] Mk 1.23, Lk 4.33.
[4] Mk 1.28. In this case the New English Bible translates *euthys* twice: 'The news spread rapidly, and he was soon spoken of'.
[5] Lk 4.37.
[6] Mk 1.29. The New English Bible translates correctly: 'On leaving the synagogue they went straight to the house of Simon and Andrew'. For the structure of the sentence see above, pp. 46f., in connection with Mk 1.10.
[7] Mt 8.14, Lk 4.38.
[8] Mk 1.30. Strangely the New English Bible here translates literally: 'They told him about her at once'.
[9] Mt 8.14ff.
[10] Lk 4.38.
[11] Mk 1.31.
[12] The New English Bible seems to follow the reading without it: 'The fever left her'.
[13] Mt 8.15.
[14] Lk 4.39; see above, p. 40.

'it left her' to 'she arose' does not seem inexplicable. No parallel in John.

Jesus told a leper to be clean, 'and at once the leprosy departed from him'.[1] The cure took place immediately, that is. Matthew and Luke both agree in this respect.[2] No parallel in John.

In the following verse Jesus 'at once dismissed him'.[3] Whether this stresses the immediacy or approximates 'duly' cannot be decided without going into the difficult background of the dismissal.[4] The notice is not represented in Matthew or Luke.[5] No parallel in John.

Jesus again went to Capernaum, his presence became known, 'and at once many were gathered together'.[6] The adverb appears only in some MSS. It denotes the immediacy of the consequence. The notice is not represented in Matthew,[7] nor really in Luke.[8] No parallel in John.

Some scribes thought him a blasphemer, 'and at once, as Jesus perceived it in his spirit that they so reasoned, he saith unto them'.[9] The immediacy is stressed: Jesus retorted before being expressly challenged. D omits the adverb. So do Matthew and Luke.[10] No parallel in John.

Jesus told a man 'Arise, take thy bed and go unto thy house': 'and he arose and at once, having taken up the bed, went out before them all'.[11] The adverb is half-way between 'immediately' and 'duly'. There is good reason why it comes, not at the beginning of the verse, but only after 'and he arose':[12] the majority of the crowd are

---

[1] Mk 1.42. The New English Bible correctly: 'The leprosy left him immediately'.

[2] Mt 8.3, Lk 5.13; see below, pp. 60, footnote 6, 63.

[3] Mk 1.43. The New English Bible: 'Then he dismissed him'.

[4] Cp. Mk 5.18f., Lk 8.38.

[5] Mt 8.4, Lk 5.14.

[6] Mk 2.2; cp. 6.54f., 7.25.

[7] Mt 9.1ff.

[8] Lk 5.17f.

[9] Mk 2.8; cp. Mk 5.30, to be discussed below, p. 53. The New English Bible suppresses the adverb. For the structure of the sentence see above, pp. 46f., in connection with Mk 1.10.

[10] Mt 9.4, Lk 5.22.

[11] Mk 2.12. The New English Bible accepts 'at once' but connects it with the wrong verb: 'took his stretcher at once and went out'. No great matter in this case, but see above, pp. 46f., in the discussion of Mk 1.10, for the structure of the sentence.

[12] See below, pp. 55f., for a similar difficulty in Mk 7.35.

outside the house, so it is only after 'and he arose' that the fully public part of the miracle takes place. Matthew omits the adverb (besides other changes).[1]

Luke, as elsewhere, replaces *euthys* by *parachrema* and places it at the beginning of the verse—but he also introduces full publicity from the first moment: 'and straightway having arisen before them, having taken up that whereon he lay, he departed'.[2] In John, at Bethesda, Jesus tells a sick man 'Arise, take up thy bed and walk'— 'and at once the man was made whole and took up his bed and walked'.[3] The scene is laid in the open, not in a house; the adverb (*eutheos*), as in Luke, stands at the beginning of the verse.

Jesus gave offence by healing on a Sabbath; 'and having gone out, the Pharisees at once took counsel'.[4] The meaning is probably half-way between 'immediately' and 'accordingly', 'in due course'. D omits the adverb, as do Matthew and Luke.[5] No parallel in John.

In the parable of the sower, some seed fell on rocky ground, 'and at once it sprang up, and when the sun was risen it was scorched'.[6] The reference is to quick, ephemeral growth. Matthew agrees,[7] Luke omits it.[8] No parallel in John.

In the interpretation of the parable the adverb occurs three times. First, the parable itself mentions seed dropped by the way side and devoured by birds. This, we learn, means: 'When they have heard, at once Satan cometh and taketh away the word'.[9] 'At once' equals 'immediately'. This is quite clear from the contrast with the next category of men, in the following verses, who at least initially take note of the word. Matthew omits the adverb,[10] Luke puts *eita*, 'then'.[11]

In the following verses, then, we are given the interpretation of the fast, ephemeral seed, and here we find *euthys* two more times: 'When they have heard the word, at once they receive it

---

[1] Mt 9.7.

[2] Lk 5.25; see above, p. 40.

[3] Jn 5.9; see below, p. 65.

[4] Mk 3.6. The New English Bible renders the sense: 'but the Pharisees, on leaving the synagogue, began plotting'.

[5] Mt 12.14, Lk 6.11.

[6] Mk 4.5. The New English Bible correctly: 'it sprouted quickly'.

[7] Mt 13.5; see below, p. 60, footnote 6.

[8] Lk 8.6.

[9] Mk 4.4, 15. The New English Bible renders the sense: 'No sooner have they heard it than Satan comes'.

[10] Mt 13.19.

[11] Lk 8.12.

with joy; and they have no root, then, when tribulation ariseth, at once they stumble'[1]. Easy come, easy go: 'at once' refers to superficial haste. The first 'at once' is omitted by D. Matthew has the adverb both times,[2] Luke not at all.[3] No parallel in John.

In the parable of the seed growing secretly, the sower is confident and patient; 'but when the fruit is ripe, at once he putteth forth the sickle'.[4] 'At once' means 'immediately', emphasizing the contrast between the time of quiet wait and the moment of action. No parallel in other gospels.

The quotation from Joel is met also in Rabbinic eschatology.[5] That might be said to be so natural as to have no relevance. But the Rabbis use it to oppose the period before ripeness to the moment of ripeness, and more than that, they use it to impress the futility of harvesting during the former and the efficiency in seizing the latter: 'If a field is reaped before its time, even its straw is no good, if at its time, it is good'.

When Jesus went ashore in the country of the Gadarenes, 'at once there met him a man with an unclean spirit'.[6] The adverb cannot be pressed, it rather means 'in due course', 'as had to happen at that stage'. It is omitted by Matthew and Luke.[7] No parallel in John.

The devils asked to be sent into the swine, 'and Jesus gave them leave at once'.[8] However, an alternative reading is 'and he gave them leave'. To establish the exact import of 'at once'—i.e. whether it means 'immediately' or 'duly'—it would be necessary to analyse the significance of request and response in this problematic episode. The adverb does not appear in Matthew or Luke.[9] No parallel in John.

---

[1] Mk 4.16f. The New English Bible renders the sense in the first half, 'as soon as they hear, they accept', and translates literally in the second, 'they fall away at once'.

[2] Mt 13.20f.; see below, p. 60, footnote 6.

[3] Lk 8.1.

[4] Mk 4.29, quoting Joel 4.13. The New English Bible renders the sense: 'but no sooner as the crop is ripe, he sets to work'.

[5] Song of Solomon Rabba on 8.14; see Stack-Billerbeck, op. cit., vol. 1, 1922, 672, vol. 4, pt. 2, 1928, 860.

[6] Mk 5.2. The New English Bible omits the adverb.

[7] Mt 8.28, Lk 8.27.

[8] Mk 5.13. The New English Bible follows the shorter reading, without 'at once'.

[9] Mt 8.32, Lk 8.32.

The woman with an issue of blood touched Jesus's garment from behind, 'and at once her blood dried up'[1]—the cure, that is, was immediate, as in other cases.[2] Matthew does not use 'at once', but (disregarding major divergences) he does say that the woman was cured 'from that hour'.[3] Luke (otherwise less divergent) substitutes *parachrema* for *euthys*.[4] No parallel in John.

In the very next verse we read: 'And at once, as Jesus perceived that virtue had gone out of him, turning him about he said'.[5] Again, emphasis on immediacy: Jesus reacted without being first told. The notice is not represented in Matthew,[6] and Luke, among other changes, omits 'at once'.[7] No parallel in John.

The New English Bible is extraordinarily emphatic as far as the cure is concerned: 'And there and then the source dried up'. By contrast, it does less than justice to Jesus's immediate discovery: 'At the same time Jesus, aware, turned round'. This is too smooth an idiom.

Jairus's daughter was reported to have died; 'but Jesus at once, overhearing the word spoken, saith, Fear not'.[8] The adverb is omitted in many MSS, but as it looks somewhat awkward and as it occupies a characteristically Marcan position,[9] the probability is that it is genuine. Anyhow it denotes immediacy, Jesus gives his assurance without first making enquiries. The incident is not represented in Matthew,[10] and Luke omits 'at once'.[11] No parallel in John.

Subsequently in this narrative, there are two more occurrences of the adverb. We are told how Jesus bade the girl arise, 'and at once she arose'.[12] The cure was immediate, as in other cases.[13] Matthew omits 'at once',[14] Luke substitutes *parachrema*.[15] No parallel in John.

---

[1] Mk 5.29.
[2] E.g. Mk 1.31, 42, above, pp. 49f.
[3] Mt 9.22; see above, p. 41.
[4] Lk 8.44; see above, pp. 40f.
[5] Mk 5.30; cp. 2.8, above, p. 50.
[6] Mt 9.22.
[7] Lk 8.45ff.
[8] Mk 5.36. The New English Bible follows the reading without 'at once'.
[9] See above, pp. 46f., in the discussion of Mk 1.10.
[10] Mt 9.18ff.
[11] Lk 8.50.
[12] Mk 5.42. The New English Bible correctly: 'Immediately the girl got up'.
[13] Cp. Mk 5.29 just discussed.
[14] Mt 9.25.   [15] Lk 8.55; see above, p. 41.

The adverb recurs very soon after: 'and they were at once astonished with a great astonishment'.[1] Here 'accordingly', 'duly', 'in the steady, continuous development of events', seems to be meant. Matthew and Luke omit it.[2] No parallel in John.

Herodias told her daughter to ask the king for the head of the Baptist; 'and having come in at once with haste she asked'.[3] Whether the meaning is nearer 'immediately'—she came while the king was still at table—or 'accordingly'—in pursuance of her mother's desire—is hard to say. D omits the adverb. Matthew makes no mention of an exit and re-entry.[4] No parallel in Luke[5] or John.

The story goes on to say that the king was sorry but could not refuse; 'and at once, having sent forth a soldier, he commanded to bring his (the Baptist's) head'.[6] The action in question here is preceded by reluctance, conflicting feelings, though finally the king decides that he has no choice. The adverb, it is evident, does not signify 'immediately'; it signifies 'accordingly', 'duly', 'as had to happen'. It is omitted by Matthew.[7] No parallel in Luke or John.

Jesus fed a multitude; 'and at once he constrained his disciples to enter into the boat, while he himself sendeth the multitude away'.[8] Probably emphasis is laid on the immediacy of the departure of the disciples, as contrasted with the staying behind of Jesus. But it may be the more general Marcan *euthys*, 'and so'. It is taken over by Matthew;[9] John has *oun* in what may be regarded as the corresponding passage,[10] but this may well have nothing to do with the adverb in Mark.

The disciples, seeing Jesus walk on the sea, think him an apparition; 'but he at once spoke with them, Be of good cheer'.[11] Probably

---

[1] Mk 5.42. The New English Bible approximates the sense by rendering: 'At that they were beside themselves'.

[2] Mt 9.26, Lk 8.56.

[3] Mk 6.25. The New English Bible correctly 'the girl hastened back at once'.

[4] Mt 14.8.

[5] Execution of the Baptist is mentioned in Lk 9.9.

[6] Mk 6.27. The New English Bible renders the sense 'So the king sent a soldier with orders'; though the peculiarly Marcan attachment of the adverb to 'he commanded' gets lost—see above, in connection with Mk 1.10, pp. 46f.

[7] Mt 14.10.

[8] Mk 6.45; cp. Mk 8.10, below, p. 56. The New English Bible: 'As soon as it was over, he made his disciples embark'.

[9] Mt 14.22; see below, p. 60, footnote 6.

[10] Jn 6.15.

[11] Mk 6.50. The New English Bible here admits 'at once'.

the word again denotes immediacy— either in the sense that Jesus lost no time in calming them or in that, that he spoke before they could take a wrong step to deal with a demon. D omits the word, and so does John;[1] but Matthew has it.[2] No parallel in Luke.

'And when they were come out of the ship, at once, knowing him, they (the people) ran through that whole region and began to carry the sick'.[3] The meaning is 'immediately', just as in the narrative of Jesus's return to Capernaum[4] or in the following text.[5] Matthew omits it.[6] No parallel in Luke or John.

Jesus's wish to remain unrecognized was in vain: 'but at once, as a woman whose daughter had an unclean spirit had heard of him, she came and fell at his feet'.[7] Immediacy, as in the text just discussed.[8] Matthew says nothing about the desire to remain unrecognized and the woman hearing about Jesus; 'at once' is omitted, but we do find 'behold', *idou*—Matthew starts 'and behold a woman came'.[9] No parallel in Luke or John.

The New English Bible strangely translates 'almost at once'. As elsewhere it connects the adverb with the wrong verb: 'Almost at once a woman heard of him, came in and fell at his feet'. In actual fact 'at once' qualifies 'she fell at his feet', in the manner explained above.[10]

A man who was deaf and suffered from a speech impediment was told by Jesus 'Be opened': 'and his ears were opened and at once the bond of his tongue was loosed'.[11] The adverb may merely mean 'and so', 'and at the same time'. It is, however, possible that it stresses the immediacy of liberation, of free expression, once Jesus's word had been able to penetrate, so that a literal translation would

---

[1] Jn 6.20.

[2] Mt 14.27; see below, p. 60, footnote 6.

[3] Mk 6.54f. The New English Bible correctly puts 'immediately' but connects it with the wrong verb: 'he was immediately recognized; and the people scoured'. For the characteristically Marcan arrangement, see above, pp. 46f., under Mk 1.10.

[4] Mk 2.2; see above, p. 50.

[5] Mk 7.25, to be discussed presently.

[6] Mt 14.35.

[7] Mk 7.25.

[8] Mk 6.54f.

[9] Mt 15.21.

[10] See pp. 46f., in connection with Mk 1.10.

[11] Mk 7.35. The New English Bible may be rendering the sense correctly: 'and at the same time'. Though when it goes on 'the impediment was removed', it eliminates important associations evoked by *elythe ho desmos*.

be best. Many MSS omit the awkward word. No parallel in the other gospels.

Jesus fed a multitude (a second time) and sent them away; 'and at once, having entered into a ship with his disciples, he came to Dalmanutha'.[1] Probably 'and in due course', though it is just conceivable that the immediacy of removal from the scene is being emphasized. Certainly no miraculously fast crossing is thought of, as in a Johannine story of a storm at sea to be inspected below.[2] Matthew omits 'at once'.[3] No parallel in Luke or John.[4]

In the story of the transfiguration, as already observed, in the ending 'and suddenly, having looked round, they saw no one save Jesus', D substitutes 'and at once', *kai eutheos*.[5] This seems a toning down to the more usual 'and in due course', 'in accordance with the course things had to take'.

Jesus joined his disciples who were surrounded by a crowd: 'and at once all the crowd, when they beheld him, were greatly amazed'.[6] Half-way between immediacy of effect and steady, necessary succession of events. The notice is not represented in Matthew[7] or Luke, though the latter, in telling how one of the crowd asked help for his son, begins 'and behold (*idou*) a man of the company cried out'.[8] No parallel in John.

One of the crowd, then, brought his son who was possessed; 'and when the spirit saw him, at once he tore him'.[9] Half-way between 'immediately' and 'as would happen'. D omits it. The notice is not represented in Matthew.[10] Luke does not depict the seizure as the demon's reaction to the sight of Jesus, and he omits *euthys*. The

---

[1] Mk 8.10; cp. 6.45, above, p. 54. The New English Bible connects *euthys* with the wrong verb, 'and without delay got into the boat'. For the right connection, see the discussion of Mk 1.10, above, pp. 46f. However, the editor who inserted *euthys* at the end of Jn 21.3 probably anticipated the misconstruction: see below, p. 65.

[2] Jn 6.21; see below, p. 66.

[3] Mt 15.39.

[4] But see below, p. 65, on a variant in Jn 21.3.

[5] Mk 9.8; see above, under *exapina*, p. 33.

[6] Mk 9.15. The New English Bible: 'As soon as they saw Jesus, the whole crowd was overcome with awe'. For the structure of the sentence, see above, pp. 46f., in connection with Mk 1.10.

[7] Mt 17.14.

[8] Lk 9.37f.

[9] Mk 9.20. The New English Bible renders the sense: 'And as soon as the spirit saw him, it threw him into convulsions'.

[10] Mt 17.14ff.

latter may well, however, have influenced his version: he emphasizes that a seizure took place just as they were bringing the patient,
'as he was yet a coming'.[1] No parallel in John.

Euthys occurs a third time in this narrative. Jesus encouraged
the father to believe; 'at once, crying out, he said, I believe'.[2] 'At
once' to be taken literally: the response was immediate. The dialo-
gue is not represented in Matthew or Luke.[3] No parallel in John.

Jesus told Bartimaeus, 'Thy faith hath made thee whole': 'and
at once he received his sight'.[4] The cure was immediate, as in other
cases.[5] Matthew agrees,[6] Luke substitutes *parachrema*.[7] No parallel
in John.

In the preparation of the entry into Jerusalem, *euthys* occurs
twice, both times pregnantly in the sense 'in due course', 'in the
appropriate succession of events'. Jesus sends two disciples into a
village, 'and at once, entering, ye shall find a colt'.[8] If the emphasis
were on immediacy, surely the adverb would be resumed a few
verses further on, where the execution of the mission is reported;
but it is not.[9] Matthew agrees—though, by ejection of the participle 'entering', the typically Marcan structure ('at once'—participle—main verb to which 'at once' belongs) is dissolved.[10] Luke
omits the adverb.[11] No parallel in John.

Jesus goes on to explain to his disciples that they are to take
the colt and, if challenged, to declare: 'The Lord hath need of him
and at once he will send him again hither'.[12] Hardly a promise of
direct return, out of keeping with the majestic demand: the meaning
must be 'in due course'. It is perhaps worth remarking that if

---

[1] Lk 9.42. In Lk 22.60, discussed above, pp. 42f., 'while he yet spake' is
coupled with a *parachrema* taking the place of a Synoptic *euthys*.

[2] Mk 9.24. The New English Bible suppresses the adverb. For the structure of the sentence, see above, pp. 46f., in connection with Mk 1.10.

[3] Mt 17.18, Lk 9.42.

[4] Mk 10.52. The New English Bible here does translate 'at once'.

[5] E.g. Mk 1.31, 42, above, pp. 49f.

[6] Mt 20.34, see below, p. 60, footnote 6.

[7] Lk 18.43; see above, pp. 41f., 49f.

[8] Mk 11.2. The New English Bible 'just as you enter'; yet in this case a
literal understanding seems inadequate. For the structure of the sentence,
see above, under Mk 1.10, pp. 46f.

[9] Mk 11.4.

[10] Mt 21.2; see below, pp. 60, footnote 6, 61.

[11] Lk 19.30.

[12] Mk 11.3. The New English Bible 'without delay', but once more we
prefer the other, typically Marcan sense.

you borrow without the owner's knowledge (Cambridge undergraduate cyclists, please note!), according to the School of Shammai you are a *gazlan*, 'thief', 'robber', according to that of Hillel a proper borrower.[1]

Matthew retains the adverb but apparently makes this part of the sentence into a prediction of the challenger's understanding; 'again' is omitted—so we get 'and at once he will send them', i.e. the challenger will allow the animals (in Matthew it is two animals) to be taken.[2] The challenger seems to have become the owner, who can confer the right to use his property. Even so, the sense may well be 'duly', as in the preceding verse 'at once ye shall find'. Luke omits the difficult clause.[3] No parallel in John.

'Behold', said Jesus, 'he that betrayeth me is at hand'—'and at once, while he yet spake, cometh Judas'.[4] Here emphasis on immediacy—Judas comes the moment Jesus announces him—and emphasis on the blow upon blow, *planmässige*, course of things coincide. The New English Bible is very wrong in introducing a break instead of stressing continuity: 'Suddenly Judas appeared'. This was anything but 'sudden'.

D omits the adverb. So do Matthew and Luke, though both, after 'while he yet spake', insert 'behold', *idou*.[5] In Luke, indeed, Jesus does not announce Judas's coming. The account in John differs.[6]

Judas had told those whom he brought that the man he would kiss would be Jesus; 'and, having come, at once, having gone up to him, he saith, Master'.[7] Half-way between 'immediately' and 'duly'. D omits it. Matthew has it;[8] though, in view of this evangelist's misconstruction of the same syntax in an earlier case,[9] it may well be that he means 'and at once having gone up to Jesus, he said'—not, as Mark, 'and at once, having gone up, he saith'. At any rate

---

[1] Bab. Baba Metzia 43b, cp. Bab. Baba Bathra 88a.

[2] Mt 21.3; see below, p. 60, footnote 6.

[3] Lk 19.31.

[4] Mk 14.43. The structure of the sentence is similar to that explained above, pp. 46f., in connection with Mk 1.10.

[5] Mt 26.47, Lk 22.47.

[6] Jn 18.3. Verse 4 contains a reference to Jesus's foreknowledge.

[7] Mk 14.45.

[8] Mt 26.49; see below, pp. 60, footnote 6, 61.

[9] Mt 3.16 misconstruing Mk 1.10, see above, p. 47. Cp. also Mt 4.20 very likely misconstruing Mk 1.18; see above, p. 48.

the New English Bible, while admitting 'at once', connects it with the wrong verb: 'he came forward at once'.

Luke omits 'at once' in pursuance of other changes: he does not say that Judas had pre-arranged the kiss.[1] The incident is not noted in John.[2]

Jesus had predicted to Peter that before the cock would crow twice he would betray him three times; Peter did deny him a first, a second, a third time—'and at once the second time the cock crew'.[3] Probably: 'in due course', no miracle in the narrow sense, just the inevitable chain of events. Matthew and John also have 'at once';[4] whereas Luke substitutes *parachrema* and adds 'while he yet spake', more in the nature of a miracle or rather, as shewn above, an immediate compliance with Jesus's prediction.[5]

Finally, 'And at once in the morning the chief priests, having consulted, having bound Jesus, carried him away and delivered him to Pilate'.[6] 'In due course', 'accordingly','as had to happen'. Neither Matthew nor Luke nor John has the adverb.[7] Matthew writes *de*, a non-committal particle, John, on the other hand, *oun*, not so remote in sense from the Marcan *kai euthys*. The New English Bible omits 'at once', thus assimilating Mark to the other Synoptics.

Weiss noted[8] that *euthys* in Mark frequently defies literal rendering, and that in many of these passages it is absent from a variant reading or the parallel version in other gospels. The conclusion he drew was that the adverb was employed by Mark on a very small number of occasions only, and that everywhere else it is due to later scribes. This goes counter to the—still sound—working hypothesis in favour of the more difficult alternative. Kilpatrick avoids this mistake.[9] But he may be too extreme in another direction. From the fact that in the vast majority of cases *euthys* comes at the be-

---

[1] Lk 22.47. In verse 48, however, such a pre-arrangement is alluded to.

[2] Jn 18.3f.

[3] Mk 14.30, 72. The New English Bible, weakly, 'Then the cock crew a second time'.

[4] Mt 26.74, Jn 18.27; see below, pp. 60, footnote 6, 67.

[5] Lk 22.60; see above, pp. 42f.

[6] Mk 15.1. For the structure of the sentence, see above, pp. 46f., in connection with Mk 1.10.

[7] Mt 27.1, Lk 22.66, Jn 18.28.

[8] Zeitschrift für die Neutestamentliche Wissenschaft 11, 1910, 124ff.

[9] The Bible Translator 7, 1958, 2f.

ginning of its clause, he infers that it is not in Mark an adverb of
time but a mere connecting particle.

However, in not a few texts the literal force of 'at once' is clear—
in most of those, for example, where Luke substitutes *parachrema*.[1]
As for the others, quite likely part of the explanation is that *euthys*
at the time may have been widely used in a reduced, worn-out
sense, as a connecting particle. But it is only part of the explanation.
Its role in Mark is too uniformly a little more than only that; a
fact underlined by cases where the position of the particle is rather
subtle, certainly not mechanical.[2] Perhaps the proper way of put-
ting it is that Mark had a reason to choose just this connecting
particle where he did—the reason being that it does express the
inevitable, one-after-the-other succession of events, from the first
temptation to the final delivering over to Pilate. There are two or
three lengthy stretches without the adverb, notably the day of
questions,[3] the Synoptic Apocalypse,[4] the passion.[5] Were these taken
over from some source or sources without much modification? Or
is it accident?

b) *Matthew*

In Matthew, the adverb appears less than half as often as in
Mark—eighteen times. That may be the reason why it is never, it
seems, omitted in variants: it is already suppressed in most of the
awkward places. In fourteen texts it appears in Mark as well as
Matthew, and we shall not dwell on them.[6] This leaves four.

Peter, walking on the water, cried for help; 'and Jesus, at once
stretching forth his arm, caught him'.[7] The meaning is 'immediately'.
The incident is not recorded in Mark or John,[8] and there is no parallel in Luke.

That the saviour should respond without delay is natural ; a

---

[1] Mk 1.31, 2.12, 5.29, 5.42, 10.52, 14.72.
[2] E.g. 'and he arose and at once went out before all' in Mk 2. 12; above,
pp. 50f.
[3] Mk 12.
[4] Mk 13.
[5] Mk 15.2 to the end.
[6] Mt 3.16 with Mk 1.10; Mt 4.20, Mk 1.18; Mt 4.22, Mk 1.20; Mt 8.3,
Mk 1.42; Mt 13.5, Mk 4.5; Mt 13.20, Mk 4.16; Mt 13.21, Mk 4.17; Mt 14.22
Mk 6.45; Mt 14.27, Mk 6.50; Mt 20.34, Mk 10.52; Mt 21.2, Mk 11.2;
Mt 21.3, Mk 11.3; Mt 26.49, Mk 14.45; Mt 26.74, Mk 14.72.
[7] Mt 14.31. The New English Bible correctly 'at once'.
[8] Mk 6.45ff., Jn 6.15ff.

rescue *eutheos* from danger at sea by Serapis is mentioned in a papyrus.[1] What is remarkable is that, at first sight, in this as in two more texts to be inspected presently, we seem to have before us the structure so greatly favoured by Mark: a participle separating 'at once' from the verb it qualifies.[2] We might interpret, that is, 'and at once Jesus, stretching forth his arm, caught him'. But Matthew probably means it the other way. Going through the four texts where Mark has his characteristic structure and *euthys* recurs in the Matthean parallel, we find that Matthew misunderstands the structure—i.e. connects the adverb with the participle—in at least one,[3] very likely two,[4] possibly three;[5] and in the fourth where he correctly connects the adverb with the main verb, he drops the participle.[6] It looks, therefore, as if, formally, in choosing the sequence 'at once'—participle—main verb, Matthew might have been influenced by the Marcan style, but that syntactically, there is a difference: in Matthew 'at once' does belong to the participle, in Mark it does not. This may be a complicated solution, but, then, the Synoptic relationships are complicated. The alternative would be to invoke some common source behind both Mark and Matthew—not only more complicated but also less plausible on other grounds.

The Synoptic Apocalypse warns of tribulations which will precede the coming of the Son of Man.[7] Then we are given a first description of his coming—it will be like lightning.[8] There follows a second description which starts: 'and at once after the tribulation of those days shall the sun be darkened'.[9] Meaning: 'immediately'. In Mark, the first description is not found. We hear of tribulations, then: 'but in those days, after that tribulation the sun shall be darkened'.[10] Luke is similar to Mark in this respect.[11] *Eutheos de* in Matthew is inserted, we conclude, in order to regain contact, across the first

---

[1] BGU 423,8 cited by Bauer, Wörterbuch zum Neuen Testament, 5th ed., 1958, 633, s.v. *eutheos*.

[2] See above, pp. 46f., the discussion of Mk 1.10.

[3] Mt 3.16, Mk 1.10, see above, p. 47.

[4] Mt 4.20, Mk 1.18, see above, p. 48.

[5] Mt 26.49, Mk 14.45, see above, p. 58.

[6] Mt 21.2, Mk 11.2, see above, p. 57.

[7] Mt 24.21ff.

[8] Mt 24.26ff.

[9] Mt 24.29. The New English Bible: 'As soon as the distress of those days has passed'.

[10] Mk 13.24.

[11] Lk 21.25.

description of the parousia, with the period of tribulation. No parallel in John.

In the parable of the talents, a man about to travel entrusted various servants with various sums of money; 'he who had received the five talents, at once going forth, traded with them'[1]. Meaning: 'immediately'—the good servant lost no time in setting to work. As in the story about Peter,[2] the structure looks Marcan and we might translate 'at once he who had received the five talents, going forth, traded with them'. But more likely Matthew connects *eutheos* with the participle.

According to a variant reading, certainly inferior, 'at once' belongs to the previous clause, concerning the master: 'and he took his journey at once'. The meaning would still be 'immediately'. That is to say, no instructions were given, the servants were left to make their own decisions.

The parallel in Luke is told quite differently.[3] No parallel in Mark or John.

Some of those who witnessed the crucifixion said that Jesus was calling Elijah; 'and one of them, at once running and taking a sponge, gave him to drink'.[4] The meaning is 'immediately': the man acted before the other bystanders expressed their different attitude.[5] The word does not appear in Mark but, then, in Mark, the man's action is not followed by an utterance of the others.[6] The accounts of Luke and John are rather different.[7]

Let us note that, as in two of the texts discussed above,[8] we might connect 'at once' with the main verb, 'gave him to drink'. But Matthew hardly intends this structure.

It emerges that where Matthew uses 'at once' independently of Mark, a literal interpretation is safest. The same, we shall see, is true of Luke. This is not in conflict with the observation that to emphasize, against Mark, the immediate fulfilment of a curse uttered by Jesus, Matthew uses *parachrema*[9].

---

[1] Mt 25.15f. The New English Bible has 'at once'.
[2] Mt 14.31.
[3] Lk 19.12ff.
[4] Mt 27.48. The New English Bible: 'at once'.
[5] Mt 27.49.
[6] Mk 15.36.
[7] Lk 23.35ff., Jn 19.28f.
[8] Mt 14.31, 25.15f.
[9] Mt 21.19f., Mk 11.11ff.; see above, p. 39.

c) *Luke*

In Luke, the adverb occurs seven times; only once in agreement with Mark—'and at once the leprosy departed from him'.[1] In one passage (which, if we counted it, would bring the total up to eight), in a saying exclusive to Luke, 'at once' is secondary: 'and no man having drunk old wine at once desireth new'.[2] *Eutheos* is not well attested; it is evidently inserted by post-Lucan editors in order to mitigate the —no doubt originally pre-Lucan—saying, which seems to recommend the old regime.[3]

He that hears Jesus but does not act on it is like one building a house without proper foundation, 'against which the stream brake and at once it fell in'.[4] Meaning: 'immediately'. D omits the word, as does Matthew—but in Matthew it would not be so fitting since he enumerates a series of assaults the house suffers before collapsing: 'and the rain descended, and the floods came, and the winds blew and smote upon that house, and it fell'.[5] Matthew is nearer to Ezekiel in this respect.[6] In a simile like this we must indeed allow for freedom in detail. In the Rabbinic models, sometimes we do find *miyyadh*, 'at once', sometimes we do not.[7] No parallel in Mark or John. Nowadays, of course, it would be acting without hearing that would be compared to building a house without foundations.

'Be like unto men looking for their lord; that when he cometh and knocketh, they may at once open to him'.[8] 'Immediately'. No direct parallel in the other gospels, but readiness is of course enjoined in Matthew and Mark.[9]

'When ye see a cloud rising in the west, at once ye say, There cometh a shower'.[10] 'Immediately'—without hesitation, genuine or affected, in contrast to their refusal to appreciate the present

---

[1] Lk 5.13, Mk 1.42; see above, p. 50.

[2] Lk 5.39; absent from Mt 9.16f., Mk 2.21f.

[3] See Lagrange, L'Evangile selon Saint Luc, 1921, 173.

[4] Lk 6.49; cp. Ja 1.23, below, p. 72. The New English Bible: 'As soon as the river burst upon it, it collapsed'.

[5] Mt 7.27.

[6] Ez 13.11ff.

[7] Strack-Billerbeck, op. cit., vol. 1, 1922, 469, gives references. *Miyyadh*, e.g., in Aboth deRabbi Nathan 24.2, 3, 4; not in 22 (equals Mishnah Aboth 3.18).

[8] Lk 12.36. The New English Bible: 'ready to let him in the moment he arrives'.

[9] E.g. Mt 24.43ff., 25.1ff., Mk 13.33ff.; see above, pp. 28ff.

[10] Lk 12.54; cp. the next text, Lk 14.5. The New English Bible: 'at once'.

crisis. That there is not overmuch emphasis on it is evident from
the following verse, where it is not resumed: 'and when ye see a
south wind blowing, ye say, There will be a scorching heat'.[1] In
the Matthean parallel the adverb does not appear—no great matter.[2]
No parallel in Luke or John.

'Which of you shall have a son (ass?) or an ox fallen into a well,
and will not at once draw him up on a sabbath day?'.[3] 'Immediately'
—in much the same application as in the text just considered: no
hesitation, genuine or affected, in contrast to the attitude they shew
when a sick man is brought before Jesus on a Sabbath. But again,
there is not overmuch emphasis, and it is not surprising that 'at
once' is absent from a parallel rhetorical question in Matthew.[4] In
another, generally comparable Lucan passage, 'at once' would indeed be out of place since it is a question, not of reaction to some
event, but of regular, customary procedure: 'Doth not each one of
you on the sabbath loose his ox or ass and lead him away to wa-
tering?'.[5]

'But who is there of you, having a servant, that will say unto
him when he is come in from the field, At once coming up sit down
to meat, and will not rather say, Make ready wherewith I may
sup, and afterward thou shalt eat?'.[6] 'Immediately'—in contrast to
delay through further work indoors before mealtime.

Whether Luke means to connect 'at once' with the participle—in
Matthew's way—or with the main verb—in Mark's—makes little
difference. Lagrange prefers attachment to the participle,[7] as does
the New English Bible: 'Come along at once and sit down'. They
may well be right. It is just conceivable—though extremely unlikely
—that we ought to connect *eutheos* with the preceding clause: 'Who
is there that will say at once, Coming up sit down, and will not
rather say'. The sense would not be greatly affected even then.

Some inferior MSS omit 'at once'. No parallel in the other gospels.

---

[1] Lk 12.55.

[2] Mt 16.2f. The authenticity of these verses is questioned; but there is
much to be said for their being genuine, and for the textual position being
the result of attempts to overcome difficulties created by them.

[3] Lk 14.5. The New English Bible: 'will he hesitate to haul him up?'—a
very apt rendering of the sense.

[4] Mt 12.11.

[5] Lk 13.15.

[6] Lk 17.7f. The New English Bible: 'at once'.

[7] Op. cit., 455.

In the Synoptic Apocalypse, we learn that there will be wars; 'for these things must needs come to pass first, but the end is not at once'.[1] Again 'at once' in the literal sense. In Matthew and Mark the word 'first' is not found, and instead of 'not at once' we find 'not yet'.[2] Exactly what the difference implies cannot here be examined.

It is not enough to say that 'at once' in Luke always means 'immediately'. What is equally interesting is that, with a single exception, where it comes from Mark,[3] it never overlaps with *parachrema*. It never, that is, describes the immediate submission to an order by Jesus or the like. Why in that one passage Luke has failed to substitute *parachrema* we cannot say. Plainly, our contention that *parachrema* has a very special meaning is strongly supported by the almost complete denial of this role to *euthys*. Our survey of Acts will lead to a similar result.

d) *John*

John uses *euthys* and *eutheos* sparingly—six times, if we discount a clause in the last chapter: 'and they entered into the boat at once'.[4] 'At once' is weakly attested. The meaning approaches that common in Mark, but found nowhere else in John: 'duly'. Probably the word was here inserted by an editor under the influence of Mark's style, especially a passage 'at once, having entered a boat with his disciples, he came to Dalmanutha'—which the editor in question no doubt understood as 'having at once entered the boat, he came'.[5]

Jesus told a lame man at Bethesda, 'Arise, take up thy bed and walk'—'and at once the man was made whole'.[6] Meaning: 'immediately'. D omits it, as does Matthew in a comparable context.[7] Mark in that context, however, does have *euthys*,[8] Luke *parachrema*.[9]

---

[1] Lk 21.9. The New English Bible correctly: 'but the end does not follow immediately'.

[2] Mt 24.6, Mk 13.7. There are other divergences looking slight but possibly significant.

[3] Lk 5.13, Mk 1.42, the first text to be discussed in this section; above, p. 63.

[4] Jn 21.3.

[5] Mk 8.10; see above, p. 56.

[6] Jn 5.9. The New English Bible: 'The man recovered instantly'.

[7] Mt 9.7.

[8] Mk 2.12; see above, pp. 50f.

[9] Lk 5.25; see above, p. 40.

The disciples, in a boat during a storm, saw Jesus walking on the sea; they were frightened, but Jesus reassured them and they were willing to take him into their boat—'and at once the boat was at the land whither they were going'.[1] Meaning: 'immediately'. This particular miracle is not met in the corresponding pericopes in Matthew and Mark; and there is no parallel in Luke. However, 'at once' repeatedly occurs in those pericopes: 'and at once he constrained his disciples to enter into the boat',[2] 'he at once spoke with them',[3] 'he at once streched forth his arm and caught him'.[4] The latter two passages are, of course, more relevant than the first if we look for a possible source of influence.

In this connection it is also worth recalling that, in Mark, after the second feeding of a multitude, Jesus 'at once, having entered into the ship with his disciples, came to Dalmanutha'.[5] In John there is only one feeding, and it is after this that the storm and miraculous crossing take place. To be sure, Mark intends no miracle.

'He then having received the sop went out at once'.[6] Meaning: 'immediately'. Whether the prompt departure takes place in obedience to Jesus's request to act quickly,[7] or as a result of the sop's and Satan's entry into Judas—the sop is mentioned four times in this brief episode[8]—or for a variety of causes, we cannot decide.

The New English Bible suppresses 'at once'. Yet it is anything but a mere connecting particle, nor does it even stand at the beginning of the sentence. Certainly John, as distinct from the Synoptics, wishes to make it unmistakably clear that Judas left at this stage, before the farewell discourses, the glorification. He reiterates the fact in opening the following section: 'When therefore he was gone out, Jesus saith'.[9] In the Synoptics it remains obscure how and when Judas detached himself.[10] John alone, too, explains how he could find the place where Jesus was arrested.[11]

---

[1] Jn 6.21. The New English Bible: 'immediately'.
[2] Mt 14.22, Mk 6.45; see above, pp. 54, 60, footnote 6.
[3] Mt 14.27, Mk 6.50; see above, pp. 54f., 60, footnote 6.
[4] Mt 14.31; see above, p. 60.
[5] Mk 8.10; see above, p. 56.
[6] Jn 13.30.
[7] Jn 13.27.
[8] Jn 13.26, twice, 27, 30.
[9] Jn 13.31
[10] Mt 26.21ff., Mk 14.18ff., Lk 22.21ff.
[11] Jn 18.2.

Towards the beginning of the farewell discourses, Jesus says: 'and at once he (God) shall glorify him (the Son of Man)'.[1] Meaning: 'immediately'. It would lead too far afield to go into the implications of this announcement. One of them may be that the cross, not a subsequent coming, constitutes the fulfilment.[2] We shall soon come across another text where immediate fulfilment is stressed.[3] No parallel in other gospels.

The New English Bible translates: 'and he will glorify him now'. This would be sound in the abstract, but it is inadequate when held together with the beginning of the speech: 'Now (*nyn*) is the Son of Man glorified'. John's subtle play on time and tense is lost if different adverbs—rare ones, too—are rendered the same way.

'Peter then denied again, and at once the cock crew'.[4] Meaning: 'immediately'. As pointed out above, both Matthew and Mark also have 'at once', whereas Luke turns it into *parachrema*.[5] Actually, the Johannine version of the cock-crow is in literal agreement with Matthew (except that John has *eutheos*, Matthew *euthys*); Mark has 'a second time', Luke 'while he yet spake', and in Luke, moreover, instead of 'the cock crew' we find 'crew the cock'. In the prediction of the incident, John essentially agrees with Luke against the others: 'The cock shall not crow till thou hast denied me thrice'.[6] However, in John, the prediction takes place in pursuance of the idea that no one can follow Jesus at this stage.[7] This may account for the absence, after the cock-crow, of any remark as to the subjective effect on Peter: the inability to follow has been objectively established and sealed—that is enough.

'But one of the soldiers pierced his side and there came out at once blood and water'.[8] Meaning: 'immediately'. We need not go into the manifold implications. It suffices to say that the miracle consists, not in the flow of blood, but in that of water. The former,

---

[1] Jn 13.32.
[2] See Bultmann, Das Evangelium des Johannes, 14th ed., 1956, 401.
[3] Jn 19.34; below, foot of this page and next page.
[4] Jn 18.27. The New English Bible renders the sense: 'and just then a cock crew'. But why it is 'a cock' here and in Lk 22.60, and 'the cock' in Mt 26.74 and Mk 14.72, is a puzzle. The Greek has the article in none of the four texts, nor in any of the four predictions.
[5] Mt 26.74, Mk 14.72, Lk 22.60; see above, pp. 42f., 59, 60, footnote 6.
[6] Jn 13.38; cp. Mt 26.34, Mk 14.30, Lk 22.34; see above, pp. 42f., 59.
[7] On the singularity of John in this matter see Daube, Novum Testamentum 5, 1962, 92f.
[8] Jn 19.34. The New English Bible: 'at once'.

if a man barely dead was stabbed, would be taken for granted;[1] the latter would be unheard of. The sequence of words bears out this conclusion: 'and water' carries the accent. This is not to deny that there may be a hint at baptism and eucharist—John excels in multivalence—but if that were the primary intention, we should get the 'correct' sequence,[2] water and blood. The primary intention goes to the miracle of the flow of water. 'There came out at once blood *and water*': the prophecies of Zechariah are realized right at this moment—'In that day there shall a fountain be opened', or 'And it shall come to pass in that day that living waters shall go forth from Jerusalem'.[3] Salvation, John means to convey, or the offer of it at least, is there. As we have just seen, an earlier passage, at the beginning of the farewell discourses, may be designed to emphasize the concept of the cross as fulfilment.[4]

A verse from this part of Zechariah is actually quoted by John in the pericope under review: 'They shall look on him whom they pierced'.[5] Both prophecies, 'In that day' and 'And it shall come to pass', as well as others referring to the waters which with the advent of the Messiah will flow from the sanctuary, figure in ancient Rabbinic exegesis.[6] There is an allusion to the second of the two prophecies in Revelation: 'And he shewed me a pure river of water of life, proceeding out of the throne of God and of the lamb'.[7] The thought of Jesus as Temple may indeed play a part in the Johannine miracle.[8]

In John, in sum, the adverb is used in six vital texts. It is used with deliberation. Its force must not be played down. The healing command of Jesus was at once obeyed.[9] Willing to receive Jesus, the disciples at once arrived at their destination.[10] Judas having received the sop at once departed.[11] Jesus announced that God would

---

[1] Cp. the Babylonian example adduced by Bauer, Das Johannesevangelium, 2nd ed., 1925, 219.

[2] For which Bauer, op. cit., 220, cites I Jn 5.6.

[3] Zech 13.1, 14.8.

[4] Jn 13.32; see above, p. 67.

[5] Jn 19.17, Zech 12.10.

[6] Tosephta Sukkah 3.9, in the main quite likely dating from New Testament times; cited by Strack-Billerbeck, op. cit., vol. 3, 1926, 854f.

[7] Rev 22.1, Zech 14.8.

[8] Cp. Jn 2.21, 4.20ff.

[9] Jn 5.9.

[10] Jn 6.21.

[11] Jn 13.30.

at once glorify him.[1] On Peter's third denial, the cock crew at once.[2] On Jesus's death his body was pierced and at once blood and water appeared.[3] The list is a tribute to John's masterly handling of vocabulary, with its apparently most negligible members becoming powerful instruments of his thought.

e) *Acts*

Ten texts in Acts, and the adverb has its literal meaning in all of them, just as in Luke.

Ananias in Jesus's name laid hands in Paul, 'and at once there fell from his eyes as it had been scales'.[4] 'Immediately'—as in the story of Peter telling Aeneas in Jesus's name to arise and make his bed, 'and at once he arose'.[5] In Luke, it may be recalled, in a passage agreeing with Mark, we found 'and at once the leprosy departed from him',[6] though in general, in cases of this type, the evangelist definitely prefers *parachrema*. In Paul's cure there is indeed a variant reading with *parachrema* in the place of *eutheos*. But as argued above this seems due to secondary interference.[7]

The adverb comes again two verses after Paul's cure. He stayed a while at Damascus 'and at once he preached Jesus in the synagogues'.[8] 'Immediately': he lost no time. There is, however, a complication. In Galatians also 'at once' occurs in the report about Paul's activity following his conversion, and here it is stated that his first step was to go to Arabia and only then he returned for a stay at Damascus: 'But when it pleased God to reveal his Son in me, that I might preach him among the heathen, at once I conferred not with flesh and blood but went into Arabia and returned again unto Damascus'.[9] A slightly different punctuation is just conceivable, but it would not affect the point here of relevance: 'that I might preach him among the heathen at once, I conferred not'.

---

[1] Jn 13.32.
[2] Jn 18.27.
[3] Jn 19.34.
[4] Acts 9.18. The New English Bible: 'immediately'.
[5] Acts 9.34.
[6] Lk 5.13, Mk 1.42; see above, pp. 50, 63.
[7] See above, p. 45.
[8] Acts 9.20.
[9] Gal 1.16. On the relation between the two reports, see e.g. Jacquier, Les Actes des Apôtres, 2nd ed., 1926, 293f.

There may well be legitimate ways of harmonizing the two accounts. But they ought not to be harmonized by weakening *eutheos* in Acts, i.e. by translating it 'at some stage not long afterwards' and reading into this an allusion to an interval spent in Arabia. (Maybe that is what the New English Bible intends with its weak rendering: 'soon he was proclaiming Jesus'. In Galatians, it does accept 'at once'.) This would be not only to ascribe to the adverb a sense it never has in Luke or Acts—nor even in Mark—but also to credit author and public with a supernatural degree of subtlety.

In a trance Peter saw a vessel descend from heaven filled with unclean beasts and he heard an order to kill and eat. 'And this was done thrice, and at once the vessel was received up into heaven'.[1] 'Immediately'—as in the story of Peter helped out of prison: 'and at once the angel departed from him'.[2] The sight displayed in a vision and the miraculous deliverer both disappear from one moment to the other: that is the very hallmark of a temporary supernatural intervention of this kind

In the former case, some inferior MSS omit *euthys,* and this variant has found defenders[3]—for no good reason. The very fact that the text sounds smoother without the adverb speaks in its favour; and so does the very similar application in the episode of Peter's liberation.

When Elymas was condemned by Paul to lose his sight for a time, 'straightway there fell on him a mist'.[4] An inferior variant replaces *parachrema* by the commoner *eutheos.* A cripple was told by Paul, 'Stand upright on thy feet'—'and he leaped up and walked'.[5] An inferior variant reads 'and at once straightway (*eutheos parachrema*) he leaped up and walked'—no doubt taking over both adverbs from other narratives of this type. We did not include these two occurrences of 'at once' above, when speaking of ten texts in Acts.

At Troas, Paul had a vision of a Macedonian asking for help: 'and when he had seen the vision, at once we sought to go forth into Macedonia'.[6] 'Immediately', in obedience to God's call. There

---

[1] Acts 10.16. The New English Bible: 'and then'.
[2] Acts 12.10. The New English Bible suppresses the adverb.
[3] Jacquier, op.cit., 319.
[4] Acts 13.11.
[5] Acts 14.10; see above, pp. 43f.
[6] Acts 16.10. The New English Bible: 'at once'.

is a variant which, in the course of a general rationalization of the account, omits the adverb.

Whether Paul and Silas were in danger at Thessalonica or whether the magistrates ordered them to leave, 'the brethren at once by night sent them away unto Beroea'.[1] 'Immediately'. The adverb is omitted in an inferior variant. The Jews at Thessalonica, however, stirred up trouble at Beroea too, 'and at once, thereupon, the brethren sent forth Paul'.[2] 'Immediately'.

A crowd dragged Paul out of the Temple 'and at once the doors were shut'.[3] 'Immediately'.

Paul, about to be scourged, invoked his Roman citizenship: 'at once, then, they which were about to examine him departed from him'.[4] 'Immediately'.

Much as in Luke, 'at once' in Acts always means 'at once'. There are two stories (in Luke there was one) where it is used in the specific sense otherwise represented by *parachrema*, namely, the cures of Paul and Aeneas.[5] Curiously, the two stories are found very close to one another. A third story might at first sight look a candidate for *parachrema*, but it is not. When Paul and his companions, moved by the former's vision at Troas, 'at once' resolved to travel to Macedonia, that was not a direct, miraculous consequence of the vision. It was a rational decision, taken by them since they were 'assuredly gathering that the Lord had called us'.[6] It was taken 'at once': they knew no hesitation in accepting the call. But it is not as if the vision had effected it *parachrema*. *Eutheos* is the right word, from the point of view of usage in Luke and Acts. The case in fact underlines that usage.

f) *Epistles and Revelation*

As for the three passages in the Epistles. We have already mentioned Galatians, apparently insisting that Paul directly after his conversion preached to the gentiles, and thus difficult to reconcile with the account in Acts.[7]

---

[1] Acts 17.10; see Jacquier, op.cit., 516. The New English Bible: 'as soon as darkness fell'.

[2] Acts 17.14. The New English Bible: 'at once'.

[3] Acts 21.30. The New English Bible: 'at once'.

[4] Acts 22.29. The New English Bible renders the sense correctly: 'withdrew hastily'.

[5] Acts 9.18, 34; cp. Lk 5.13, above, pp. 63, 65.

[6] Acts 16.10.

[7] Gal 1.16, Acts 9.20; see above, pp. 69f.

According to James, a man who hears the word but does not act on it is like one who observes his face in a mirror 'and goeth his way and at once forgetteth what manner of man he was'.[1] The meaning is 'immediately'—this passing sight does not stay in the mind at all. (The shadowy character of the image itself may also influence the choice of simile.) What the author wishes to convey is that only by doing is the word kept alive, its impression made lasting.

The author of III John finishes by saying that instead of writing he hopes 'at once to see thee'.[2] Quite apart from the fact that in concluding phrases of letters a good deal of irregular grammar and meaning is apt to creep in—we know too little of the situation to decide which is more plausible, a literal interpretation, 'immediately', or a vaguer, 'shortly', 'very soon'. Perhaps rather the latter.

Lastly, Revelation. 'A door opened in heaven, and the voice as it were of a trumpet talking with me, Come up hither. At once (and at once?) I was in the spirit'.[3] 'Immediately': a miraculous transposition.

5. MORE DEFINITION

The sudden event is unexpected, swift, startling; we might speak of a striking discontinuity. To take the three attributes in reverse order, we have repeatedly insisted on the third. A supernatural intervention may terminate as swiftly as it begins, but, as pointed out in the discussion of Mark's transfiguration,[4] since in general its beginning takes you aback far more than its termination, it is to the former that the qualification 'sudden' normally attaches. A theft may be totally unexpected but, as pointed out in the discussion of a warning of the last judgment in I Thessalonians,[5] since it does not startle (though, to be sure, the news of it may), it is not described as 'sudden'. Speed and suddenness are near enough for the Hebrew noun *regha'*, 'moment', to be used in elevated Old Testament speech in the sense of 'suddenly'. But in English,

---

[1] Ja 1.23; cp. Lk 6.49, above, p. 63. The New English Bible: 'very soon'. This is a far more responsible, cautious, scholarly statement: but it is not James.

[2] III Jn 14. The New English Bible may well give the correct sense: 'very soon'.

[3] Rev 4.2. The New English Bible: 'at once'.

[4] Mk 9.8; see above, pp. 32f.

[5] I Thess 5.3; see above, p. 29.

for example, 'in a moment' never quite has that sense. (On the other hand, the noun 'start', which may still signify 'sudden move', at one time signified also 'moment'; how the two uses are related must be left open.) Nor has *regha*ʿ that sense in post-Biblical Hebrew. Nor has the phrase 'twinkling of an eye' that sense; it will be discussed below.[1] It would not do to curse an enemy, 'May he lose health and fortune in the twinkling of an eye'.

Speed is allied to suddenness in various ways; three of them may be mentioned. First, if you wish to achieve suddenness, an unexpected stroke, you may have to proceed speedily—otherwise your plan may become known. The Gibeonites, besieged, asked Joshua to their aid 'quickly' (Hebrew *mehera*, LXX *tachos*), and his 'sudden' attack on the besiegers took place after a night march.[2] Of course, there is no speed of this kind where you do not plan; say, you kill somebody without intent, 'suddenly'.[3] Nor, by the same token, where impersonal forces produce the suddenness. God indeed need not hurry even if he plans a sudden intervention.[4]

Secondly, in early literature, where the sudden is always a catastrophe, speed may be a consequence of it—you run away in a panic. We observed above that *bhl* is among the roots characteristically in the neighbourhood of suddenness:[5] it signifies 'terror' and, in the later sources, 'haste'. Some texts listed by the dictionaries under the latter sense perhaps still shew a trace of the former: they refer to haste in the service or at the word of a king.[6] In one passage the causative *hibhhil* is used of the priests 'hurrying out' King Uzziah when, in the act of usurping their functions in the sanctuary, he was smitten with leprosy.[7]

Above all, thirdly, the sudden event itself is swift, altering the situation in no time. One could not say, 'In the course of the 20th century the Empire experienced a sudden reversal of fortune', however unexpected and startling the change might have been. The LXX, translating the Psalmist's wish that his enemies be

---

[1] See pp. 76f.

[2] Jo 10.6, 9; see above, p. 3.

[3] Nu 35.22; see above, p. 3.

[4] E.g. Nu 6.9, Lk 2.13—the idea of speed of the kind in question is definitely not present; see above, pp. 3, 30.

[5] See pp. 11, 19.

[6] Ec 8.3, Esth 2.9, 6.14, 8.14, Ezra 4.23 (equals I Esdras 2.30). See above, p. 19, footnote 5.

[7] II Chr 26.20.

ashamed 'in a moment', has *dia tachous*, 'quickly'.[1] The same
phrase is employed in Sirach, with regard to the 'sudden' turn for
the better to be hoped for by a poor who is pious.[2] In Lamentations,
sinful Sodom is overthrown 'as in a moment' in the Hebrew, *hosper
spoudei* in the LXX.[3] Luther frequently renders 'suddenly' as
schnell, 'quickly'; for example in the Lucan warning lest *komme
dieser Tag schnell über euch*.[4] We have already drawn attention to
regha', 'moment', in the sense of 'suddenly'.[5]

It might indeed be argued that, as a rule, the outcome, the
culmination, of a gradual process may be anticipated; and that
accordingly, swiftness and unexpectedness are more or less the
same, or two sides of a medal—the former an objective attribute
of the event, the latter the subjective state of the person affected.
However, there is something to be said for separate headings.

As for unexpectedness, this is essential and its importance, in
early times especially but still today, reflects man's awareness of
his limitations, his being in the hands of forces he cannot direct.
However, the unexpected that is not swift and striking at the same
time is not 'sudden'. If on waking up I find the sun shining, contrary to the pessimistic weather forecast, it is not a case of 'suddenness'. The unexpected news of Miss X's engagement to Mr Y may
or may not be 'sudden' according as I have reason to be shocked
or no.

Unexpectedness is relative. Within the general scheme of things,
any person is liable to die at any moment. Yet that is not how life
affects us: the Pentateuch speaks of a Nazarite being with a man
and that man 'suddenly' dying.[6] What is meant is that, at that
particular moment, that contingency had not entered into the
Nazarite's calculations. The pious poor is encouraged to trust that
God will 'suddenly' make him rich.[7] The unexpected 'sudden' may
be embedded, that is, within a wider framework of expectation; and
the framework need not always be so wide as in the case of liability
to death or the justice of God. If I tinker with the electric

---

[1] Ps 6.11; see above, pp. 9, 12f.
[2] Si 11.21, only in the Greek; see above, pp. 8, 12.
[3] Lam 4.6; see above, pp. 9f., 12.
[4] Lk 21.34; see above, p. 28.
[5] See pp. 9, 72.
[6] Nu 6.9; see above, pp. 3, 11.
[7] Si 11.21, in the Greek; see above, p 8.

switch, my friends know what will be the result, yet when the lights go out it may strike them as 'sudden'.

Unless we bear this relative nature of unexpectedness in mind, we may find difficulty where none exists. Malachi preaches: 'Behold I will send my messenger and he shall prepare the way, and the Lord shall suddenly come to his temple'.[1] We have already cited Rabbinic texts trying to eliminate the contradiction that though the way is prepared, the coming is sudden; of modern commentators Powis Smith notices the problem.[2] The point, however, is that general preparation does not preclude 'suddenness' of the coming in the sense that you are seized unawares at the particular moment. In the Synoptics, we are enjoined to watch 'at all time':[3] the only way to guard against that threat.

The story of Paul and the viper gains in interest if this aspect is appreciated.[4] When Paul had, as the islanders thought, been bitten by a viper, they 'expected, *prodokao*, him to be fated, *mello*, to swell up or suddenly, *aphno*, fall down dead'; and they went on doing so 'for a long time', *poly*. The general expectation that something terrible would happen was there; but they were quite prepared (maybe there is here a trace of a suggestion that that would be the way of barbarians) to be startled and accept it as 'sudden', at the particular moment and in the particular form it would occur.

6. Stigme chronou and ripe ophthalmou

Little need be said about *en stigmei chronou* in Luke: according to Luke—though not Matthew—the devil shewed Jesus all kingdoms of the world 'in a pinpoint of time'.[5] We saw that *stigme* represents *petha‛*, 'suddenly', in the LXX, in a prophecy of disaster by Isaiah;[6] it will occur in Hebrew *lephetha‛ pith'om*, in the LXX *hos stigme parachrema*. In Luke, there is nothing sudden about the display. Indeed, a comparison of the two cases is useful in bringing out plainly that what happens in a 'pinpoint', moment, may, but need

---

[1] Mal 3.1; see above, pp. 4f.
[2] See above, pp. 23f.
[3] Lk 21.36.
[4] Acts 28.3ff.; see above, pp. 29f.
[5] Lk 4.5, Mt 4.8.
[6] Is 29.5; see above, pp 4, 12.

not, be sudden. No suddenness in II Maccabees either, where *stigme* is applied in yet a different way: Antiochus's pains increased *kata stigmen*, 'every moment'.[1]

As the dictionaries shew, Luke's wording is perfectly normal; and there is no indication that he is alluding to, or under the influence of, any particular text or area of doctrine.

There is more specific history behind Paul's assurance that 'we shall be changed in a moment, in the twinkling of an eye'.[2] Whether or not he might have put 'suddenly' is a matter for speculation. Very likely he might, but the fact is, he does not. That is to say, he is here concentrating not on the awe-inspiring aspect, nor on the astonishment experienced at that juncture, but on the hope which will materialize in an instant when God so decrees.

The expression he employs is a double one. The first half, *en atomoi*, is consonant with general Greek usage; in fact Aristotle repeatedly speaks of *atomon* in a discussion of change.[3] At the same time it is safe to assume that Paul has in mind the Hebrew *regha'*, 'moment'. The phrase *en atomoi* is preserved in only one other Biblical text, namely, in Symmachus's translation of Isaiah, and there it renders *regha'*.[4]

The second half, *en ripei ophthalmou*, is a *hapax legomenon*, met nowhere else either in the Bible or any other writing. That it represents a Hebrew phrase *hereph 'ayin*, both in sense and even, to some extent, in sound (*ripe—hereph*), was noticed nearly a hundred years ago by Siegfried and Levy.[5] But what caused Paul's choice of precisely this phrase which, even in Hebrew, is not too common? For one thing, it is relevant to note that the Rabbis define *regha'* as *hereph 'ayin*: 'How long is a moment? As a twinkling of an eye'.[6] So the two halves of Paul's double expression belong traditionally together.

---

[1] II Mac 9.11; see above, p. 18.
[2] I Cor 15.52. Contrast the description in I Thess 4.13ff.
[3] E.g. Physics 6.5.235f. The word for 'change', it is true, is *metaballo*.
[4] Is 54.8. At first sight it looks as if it corresponded to Hebrew *besheṣeph*, but this is deceptive. It corresponds to *regha'*, just like Theodotion's *pros oligon*—on which latter see Field, Originis Hexapla, vol. 2, 1875, 536 n. 19.
[5] Siegfried, Analecta Rabbinica ad Novum Testamentum, 1875, 9, Jacob Levy, Wörterbuch über die Talmudim und Midraschim, vol. 1, 1876, 495, s.v. *hereph*.
[6] Jer. Berakoth 2d, Lam Rabba on 2.19; see Strack-Billerbeck, op. cit., vol. 2, 1924, 156.

For another thing, *hereph 'ayin* seems to have had a place in eschatological exposition already before Paul, besides being employed generally where the rapidity of God's power of succour is stressed.[1] A verse from Psalm 46 deserves attention: 'Be still (LXX: *scholasate*)—or, desist (Symmachus: *easate*)— and know that I am God'.[2] The Rabbis connect the whole psalm with the last things, both because its contents naturally lend themselves to such exegesis and because its authors are the sons of Korah, who did not die, Scripture says,[3] never quite died, according to the Rabbis, and therefore possessed much knowledge not accessible to ordinary mortals. In the opening, 'a song upon Alamoth' is variously understood as 'a song upon hidden things' (LXX: *hyper ton kryphion*) or 'a song upon worlds'—i.e. the two worlds assigned in the judgment to the righteous and the wicked.[4] The line 'Therefore will we not fear though the earth be removed' is said to imply that, when God renews the world, the righteous ones, resurrected, will receive eagle's wings and so forth—they will be changed.[5]

In the verse 'Be still' etc., the part 'and know that I am God' is invariably considered as envisaging final judgment or deliverance. The first word, 'be still' or 'desist', in Hebrew is *harpu*. The way it was pronounced—or at least widely pronounced—may be gathered from a transliteration extant in the Hexapla, *uarphu*. The Rabbis see here an allusion to *hereph* and, in their usual manner, credit *harpu* at once with its literal meaning and that of *hereph 'ayin*, 'twinkle of an eye'. Thus according to one view the verse means 'Desist from evildoing and do penitence but for the twinkling of an eye, and redemption will come'.[6] That punning interpretations of this sort go back a long way is certain: Aquilas renders *harpu* as *iathete*, 'be healed',[7] presupposing a Hebrew *heraphe'u*.

---

[1] Gen Rabba on 24.10; other supernaturally swift actions are also characterized by this phrase, e.g. Song of Solomon Rabba on 3.6.

[2] Ps 46.11.

[3] Nu 26.11.

[4] Midrash Psalms on 46.1; Strack-Billerbeck, vol. 4, pt. 2, 1928, 1039.

[5] Bab. Sanhedrin 92a f., cp. Midrash Psalms on 46.3; see Strack-Billerbeck, vol. 2, 1924, 255, vol. 3, 1926, 481, 845.

[6] Pesiqta 163b, Song of Solomon Rabba on 5.2: Resh (Simon ben) Laqish, middle of 3rd century A.D., and R. Levi, second half of 3rd century. See Strack-Billerbeck, vol. 1, 1922, 163—where, however, the translation *in einem Augenblick*, ' in a moment', should be corrected into *einen Augenblick*, 'for a moment'. For a similar mistranslation of Si 40.6 by the Handwörterbuch, see above, p. 10.

[7] The variant *ilasthete* is probably a development from this.

7. A GHOST

In conclusion we would lay a ghost walking the most reputable dictionaries. In the first half of the last century Gesenius, in his Thesaurus,[1] explained *petha'*, 'suddenly' — and *pith'om*, treated as an outgrowth of it—as deriving from *pathah*, 'to open'. The basic meaning was 'an opening of the eyes', hence 'a moment of time', 'suddenly'. He adduced the German *Augenblick* as a parallel. If this were correct, *petha'* would anticipate by about a thousand years the Rabbinic and Pauline 'twinkling of an eye' (though this is not, we saw, synonymous with 'suddenly'). Nothing *a priori* exceptionable in this; only it just does not happen to be the case.

There are three steps. First, the derivation from *pathah*: implausible. Second (if we grant the first), the assumption that the specific 'opening' which via 'moment' led to 'suddenly' must be of the eyes. But why ever should this be so? Third (if we grant the first two), the parallel *Augenblick*. *Augenblick*, however, in the sense of 'fraction of time', has a very different history. In fact it is on the cards that it was Luther's rather literal translation of Paul's *ripe ophthalmou* by *Augenblick*[2] which stimulated this application of the word in German.

One suspects that Gesenius's theory concerning *petha'* is really due to the influence on him of that use of the German *Augenblick*. Modern authorities no longer pay any attention to this theory, presumably because step one, the derivation from *pathah*, is rejected. They do, however, carry on his theory concerning *regha'*, which he doubtless equally formulated under the spell of *Augenblick*.

Regha' he derived from *ragha'*, 'to agitate'. Its basic meaning was 'nod of an eye', hence 'a moment of time'. Parallel: *Augenblick*.[3] (The further specialisation to 'suddenly' he did not discuss—and it is indeed, as pointed out above,[4] readily intelligible.) This view is generally approved, with the embellishment, apparently, that the Latin *momentum*, from *movere*, is also held to have reached the sense of 'fraction of time' via 'twinkling of an eye': yet another parallel.[5] Once again , we are presented with an anticipation of the Rabbinic-Pauline phrase.

---

[1] Vol. 2, fasc. 2, 1840, 1140f.
[2] I Cor 15.52; cp. *in brahva augins* in the Gothic version.
[3] Thesaurus, vol. 3, fasc. 1, 1843, 1264.
[4] See p. 9.
[5] E.g. Handwörterbuch, 744f., doubtfully, Koehler, 874, firmly.

This time the first step, though far from certain, is not untenable. The chief reason we regard it as uncertain is that *ragha'*, 'to agitate', occurs twice only, of God who 'agitated the sea and the waves roared': once in Deutero-Isaiah and once in Jeremiah.[1] This is a slender foundation to build on. Not to mention the difficulty of constructing a bridge from 'agitation' to 'fraction of time', not quite the same as from 'movement' to 'fraction of time'. Still, the derivation is obviously better than that of *petha'* from *pathah*.

The second step is completely arbitrary. Why (granting the first) should the 'agitation' accounting for *regha'*, 'moment', be of the eye? As for step three, we have already noted that *Augenblick*, far from supplying a parallel, may owe the prevalence of its sense of 'moment' to Paul.

The recent, fourth step, the forcing of the Latin word into the same scheme, is amusing. There is no longer any thought for the evidence, readily accessible in the Thesaurus Linguae Latinae. The scheme has developed —shall we say?—its own momentum.

Certainly, if (as is barely conceivable, despite the lack of any testimony) *ragha'*, 'to agitate', was widely employed in the sense of 'to move'; and if *regha'*, 'moment', evolved from this use; we may, though even then we need not, have before us a development resembling that from *movere* to *momentum* as denoting 'a fraction of time'. But neither the Hebrew nor the Latin has anything to do with a 'twinkling of an eye'.

In his Handwörterbuch,[2] earlier than his Thesaurus, Gesenius ascribed the meaning 'to nod with the eye' to the verb *ragha'* itself; the passages in Deutero-Isaiah and Jeremiah he translated 'calmed (by his nod) the sea when its waves roared'. From this starting-point, we should indeed arrive with ease at *regha'*, 'wink', 'moment', *Augenblick*. But there is little to be said for the starting-point. In the Handwörterbuch, already Gesenius claimed an analogy between the Hebrew and the Latin development, but it does not look as if he had thought it very close, i.e. as if he had considered *momentum* to be a movement of the eye. The dominant inspiration was the German *Augenblick*.

---

[1] Is 51.15, Jer 31.55. Job 26.12 may have to be added.
[2] 1828, 763f.

INDEX OF REFERENCES